MW01144724

THE RUMBLING ISLAND

Zai Whitaker is the author of many books on natural history and environmental issues, including *The Snakes Around Us*, *Andamans Boy* (Tulika), *Cobra in my Kitchen* (Rupa), *Salim Ali for Schools* (Permanent Black) and *The Boastful Centipede and Other Creatures in Verse* (Puffin). She teaches at the Kodaikanal International School. She is a Trustee of the Madras Crocodile Bank, and a board member of the Irula Women's Society.

THE RUMBLING ISLAND

TRUE STORIES FROM THE FORESTS OF INDIA

Edited by
Zai Whitaker

Illustrated by
Uma Krishnaswamy

PUFFIN BOOKS

PUFFIN BOOKS
Published by the Penguin Group
Penguin Books India Pvt. Ltd, 11 Community Centre, Panchsheel Park,
New Delhi 110 017, India
Penguin Group (USA) Inc., 375 Hudson Street, New York, New York 10014,
USA
Penguin Group (Canada), 90 Eglinton Avenue East, Suite 700, Toronto,
Ontario, M4P 2Y3, Canada (a division of Pearson Penguin Canada Inc.)
Penguin Books Ltd, 80 Strand, London WC2R 0RL, England
Penguin Ireland, 25 St Stephen's Green, Dublin 2, Ireland (a division of
Penguin Books Ltd)
Penguin Group (Australia), 250 Camberwell Road, Camberwell, Victoria
3124, Australia (a division of Pearson Australia Group Pty Ltd)
Penguin Group (NZ), 67 Apollo Drive, Rosedale, North Shore 0632,
New Zealand (a division of Pearson New Zealand Ltd)
Penguin Group (South Africa) (Pty) Ltd, 24 Sturdee Avenue, Rosebank,
Johannesburg 2196, South Africa

Penguin Books Ltd, Registered Offices: 80 Strand, London WC2R 0RL,
England

First published in Puffin by Penguin Books India 2008
This anthology copyright © Penguin Books India 2008
Introduction copyright © Zai Whitaker 2008

Copyright for the individual pieces vests with the authors
Illustrations copyright © Penguin Books India 2008

All rights reserved

10 9 8 7 6 5 4 3 2 1

ISBN: 9780143330110

Typeset in Sabon MT by Eleven Arts, Keshav Puram, Delhi 110035

Printed at Pauls Press, New Delhi

For my sons Nikhil and Samir,
with thanks for everything.

Contents

Contents

Acknowledgements

Some parts of the article by Monica Jackson are from her contribution to *India Magazine* in October 1992. Cliff Rice's piece on the Nilgiri tahr is similarly based on two articles: *India Magazine* of March 1988, and *Sanctuary Magazine* Vol. V, No. 2. Another version of Ian Lockwood's article appeared in *Sanctuary Asia*, February 2003. Thanks are due to Sanctuary Features for the use of Bittu Sahgal's article. 'The Magic Ring' is a chapter from the book *Salim Ali for Schools*, published by Permanent Black in 2003.

Introduction

This book is a collection of Indian natural history writings. When the publishers asked me to put it together, I yawned. It seemed like such a boring task. But I was quite wrong; I've enjoyed the experience thoroughly, and learnt a lot as well.

I started by making a list of naturalists who are also good writers. The first choice was of course Dr George Schaller, but I was sure he'd say no, because he's such a busy person. He's in Tibet one day, and in London the next, and in South America the third. His travel schedule reads like the itinerary of a magic carpet. Imagine my surprise when he replied immediately that he would contribute to the book, and soon after came his wonderful article. He must have written it on a plane, on his way to China to save pandas. I recalled the saying: 'If you want something done soon, ask a busy man.'

Well, all the contributors are very busy people, but they've been cooperative and prompt, and forgiven my dreadful emailing skills. I am very grateful to them for taking time off their busy schedules to create this book. I'm sure you will enjoy it, whether you're young or un-young . . . And anyway, what do those words really mean? I know some very young grandmothers who are lively and spirited and enjoy learning … and some rather old youngsters who aren't interested in anything beyond their noses. This book is full of the kind of 'true fiction' that people of all ages love. Each one of the articles takes us on a very special and unique journey.

It has been a unique journey for me as well. I've re-discovered, for instance, that naturalists don't seem to have the proper amounts of caution and fear. They think, for example, that sitting in a cave with wild tigers is perfectly normal, which of course it's not. Another abnormality is that they never give up. This is lucky for us, because otherwise many more species would be extinct today. Each one of the writers in this book has contributed to the preservation of India's wildlife and forests in different and remarkable ways. Their research and field studies have helped conserve animal, bird and plant species; their photographs and words have publicized the plight of forests and wildlife; their committees and campaigns have made our government take important actions, such as creating national parks and sanctuaries. Two of the pieces are about M. Krishnan and Salim Ali, who played key roles in Indian conservation.

Naturalists have no national or international boundaries. Our group of contributors are not all Indian. India's conservation movement owes an enormous debt to many, many naturalists from other countries. Some, like Ian Lockwood, are 'honorary Indians' who seem to be as comfortable in India as in their own country. Ian grew up in Bangladesh and south India and his photographs of the Western Ghats are absolutely amazing. Monica Jackson speaks Kannada and loves this country as much as her own. But there are, unfortunately, people who feel that 'foreigners' shouldn't be allowed to study our wildlife and forests. This is a very narrow-minded view, and an extremely ignorant one. If it wasn't for Cliff Rice, the Nilgiri tahr would never have got the global attention and resultant protection. Similarly, George Schaller's path-breaking study of the tiger in Kanha National Park revealed information that helped make plans for its conservation. Sally Walker started the Zoo Outreach Organisation which helps our zoos breed endangered species in captivity. In recent months, almost a hundred gharial have died on the Chambal from chemical-related poisoning. Reptile experts from other countries have helped identify the problem. The government has been welcoming, and grateful. Indian wildlife and forest experts are much in demand in other countries, to advise on conservation issues. This is truly the way to go. The global ownership of natural resources calls for this kind of international cooperation.

Another point of heated debate in wildlife conservation circles is whether big business houses and multinational companies should be allowed to fund and organize conservation projects. Some people feel that since these corporates often pollute the air, water and soil, they should stay away from the conservation arena and leave this work to the government. But is this a valid argument? Does the government always do what it's supposed to do? Doesn't it generate pollution as well? And—importantly—does it always have the resources? Time and again, a big hotel or company has offered to step in and clean up a lake, or regrow a forest, or create and run a wildlife sanctuary… and been discouraged by local conservationists. These people have to think hard about whether they are doing the right thing.

There's another lively debate in the conservation arena. It is the battle, often almost a war, between two armies of people with very different approaches to conservation. One army believes in total protection. They think that our natural wealth should be left alone and not used at all. The other side says that the only way to preserve our wildlife and forests is to use them. This is called 'sustainable development' and includes the collection of forest produce, farming and ranching of animals like crocodiles and deer, and limited hunting in a few protected areas. Maybe the answer lies between these two extremes. Certainly our 'total protection' policy isn't working. Our beloved tiger and lion may be extinct very soon.

As more and more forest disappears, the animals have nowhere to go. Recently, a newspaper photograph showed a herd of elephants in the middle of Bhubaneshwar town! Leopards are visiting homes and gardens in search of food. One was captured in a house outside Delhi; another carried away someone's dog near Chinglepet in Tamil Nadu; a third parked itself in a garden in Panjim, Goa. In Kodaikanal, where I live, the bison, or gaur, have come to town. Last week there were twenty-eight on Bear Shola Road; another five or six have settled in a compound not far from the busy market area. Let's face it, we're in for a difficult time as wild animals move into our habitat. It's only fair, since we've taken over theirs.

But there has been much good news as well. More and more people are setting out with binoculars to watch and study birds. Many new Protected Areas have been set up in the last decade. Forest officials and police are getting better and better at finding and arresting wildlife poachers and smugglers. Wildlife conservation organizations are springing up like mushrooms all over the country.

And, most important, the wild places of India are as beautiful as ever, so let's enjoy them. The enjoyment of natural beauty is something like a spiritual experience; it creates peace and calm and hope, and a sense of balance. Recently, I stood on a rock overlooking a shola, a type of rainforest typical of the Western Ghats. A Nilgiri langur called from deep within the thick tree canopy. Closer by, a Malabar squirrel bounded away with a loud alarm call. Overhead, two serpent eagles circled their pristine forest homeland. I gathered the sights and sounds on my memory chips, and clicked 'Save'. They would see me through the next week or two, reminding me that there is something beyond petty human anxieties and problems… something vast and wonderful and very, very comforting.

Zai Whitaker

Two Years with the Nilgiri Tahr

Cliff Rice

'Thank you, God,' I thought, 'thank you for making everything work out so well.' It really had worked out amazingly well! First, my professors had supported my proposal to study the Nilgiri tahr for my doctoral thesis, agreeing that we needed to know more about this unique ungulate's natural history and biology. Next, conservation organizations had given me funds for the project and the right officials had granted permission to camp for two years in the High Range mountains of Kerala. Moreover, I was able to stay in a small cabin by a beautiful stream in Eravikulam National Park, one of the last strongholds of the Nilgiri tahr of which only about two thousand were left. The icing on the cake was the help and hospitality offered by Vaguvarrai Tea Estate, which adjoins the national park. Now, as I climbed through the last of the tea bushes and into the park, estate workers carried my luggage on the two-hour trek.

But my gratitude didn't last too long. 'Thank you, God,' I had thought, but I was to take it all back. Suddenly, the hill above me disappeared in a low swirl of mist and rain-filled cloud. Sheets of rain crackled against my knapsack and stung my face. I tried to decipher our route through the thudding greens and thundering greys. As we climbed up to the rolling plateau, we were fully exposed to the monsoon winds sweeping across from the west; winds I would get to know very well during the remainder of the monsoon. Crossing the ridges, the wind pushed and shoved, and it seemed in the roaring whiteness that there was no God, but that the devil himself was beating me on the back with great gusts.

I often wondered, during that first monsoon, whether I would have any success at all in my study. Yes, the tahr were there; but years of being hunted had made them shy, and they took off as soon as I came into view. The thick mist didn't help. I was getting tired of the long, fruitless trudges through mist and rain. My only reward was grey shapes disappearing into the mist. And this time of the year, the monsoon, was crucial for my study because it was the rutting and mating season. I did some hard thinking, and came up with a new plan.

I decided that this monsoon was a dead loss, but I had to achieve close-range viewing of tahr by the next one. They would have to get used to my presence and the best way to do this was to drop my secretive ways and let them accept me as part of the landscape. I stopped slinking and snooping around. I let them see me in the open and waited patiently for signs that they were becoming more tame and approachable. But it was ten long months before I noticed the slightest change in their attitude. And even so, their 'flight distance' was still too long, and the monsoon was approaching. So I decided to bribe the tahr.

Like many ungulates, tahr have a great liking for salt. I started putting out salt for them. I also carried it around, and it made a big difference; suddenly, I was a lot more popular. Animals which had previously let me within 50 metres at most came right up to me to get salt. We had daily salt sessions of an hour or two. After a while, the tahr became so tolerant that I could even approach them and walk among them *without* the salt. Now, I was able to slip colour-coded collars on them and thus recognize individual animals. Life was suddenly much better, and my study began in earnest.

Soon after the monsoon on a fine, clear morning I was sitting on a rise overlooking a herd of about ten or twelve tahr, including some young ones. I knew, from the behaviour of the adults, that there was a leopard in the small ravine. The tahr were making excited sounds, halfway between a whistle and a sneeze. Then the leopard appeared, and I saw the cause of their alarm: in its jaws was a young tahr, being dragged along between the predator's forelegs.

I never again saw a leopard catch a tahr. They tried, but had little chance of out-running their prey on the steep terrain.

To my surprise, the tahr did not flee when a leopard was seen, but simply kept it under strict watch, often from as close as a dozen meters. Obviously, I was considered more dangerous than a leopard, because at the onset of the study they would take off even if I appeared at a considerable distance!

Leopards were not the only threat to the tahr at Eravikulam. Wild dogs or dhole also visited the highlands. They are skilled predators despite their small size, because they hunt in packs and can kill an animal almost ten times larger than any one of them. The regular dhole pack in my study area was nine-strong, but packs of two or three dozen have been reported elsewhere. The Eravikulam pack roamed widely on the plateau and often appeared at unexpected moments, surprising both the tahr and myself. Such was the case one day when I was in the middle of breakfast. The pack appeared on the open slope opposite my cabin and chased down, killed and consumed a female tahr and two kids, effectively postponing my own meal while I stopped to take notes.

Humans are also a threat to the Nilgiri tahr. In spite of being a protected species, poachers continue to hunt them. Some use domestic dogs to chase the tahr onto cliffs and keep them there until the poacher can approach and shoot them with his muzzleloader or shotgun. Wire snares are another, and more cruel, way of killing tahr. But, as far as I know, tahr are no longer killed with banana leaves. Regular tahr-escape routes used to be covered with banana leaves, causing them to slip and fall to their deaths.

So my study continued through the winter. Then one day,

after five months of fairly clear weather, the easterly breezes died and a listless pause descended on the plateau . . . I knew what was to follow. It was as if some huge mythical giant in the west had been inhaling steadily and was now poised to give the big blow. And in a couple of days the big blow came. With it came the tempest, flying rain and mist and low clouds streaking across the plateau. I had to lean into the wind with the rain hammering down on me, or stagger against the buffeting back currents as I made my way across some lee slope. It was often best to crawl on all fours when crossing ridge crests, and not risk being blown clean off my feet.

Now, my efforts of the past eight months paid high dividends. I could walk among the tahr in the thick monsoon mist and haze, watching them get ready to breed and produce kids. The 'rut' began; and males started competing for females. I watched several dramatic rutting sequences. Fights usually started with two males approaching each other at an angle for a dramatic clashing and bashing of horns. They would then stand side by side but facing opposite directions, and push with their shoulders and strike with their horns on the opponent's flanks. Eventually, one male would decide he had had enough. He would run off, and be seen on his way by the victor who chased him well out of the group before turning his attention to the female.

Most tahr groups had several males of various ages, and the younger ones had a hard time getting dates. The older ones kept an eye on them, and if they got too interested in a female, they were put in their place. The youngsters had to wait their turn until the older ones started seriously 'going out' with a female. They then became too preoccupied to care about the others. But before that time, there was tension in the air, and I watched several fights between males who were after the same female. One particularly stands out in my memory.

The two males involved were Wybl, named after the colour coding on his collar (white, yellow, blue), and DCH, short for Double Chip, from the two chips on his left horn. Wybl was with the female he had mated with the day before, when DCH's appearance seemed to put him in a bad mood. Wybl stared intently at him, then bent and sprayed himself with his own urine. Kneeling, he stabbed and tore the grass with his horns. DCH, who was actually courting another female and didn't seem too interested in Wybl's lady love, rose to the occasion and stared and dug up grass in return. After half an hour of this staring and tearing grass, Wybl moved towards DCH, head down and mane bristling. He moved forward in short mincing steps. Not to be outdone, DCH adopted the same posture. They came together and the fight started with clashing heads and blows on the flanks.

There is a popular conception that animals restrain themselves when fighting to avoid injuring each other, but this fight was serious. I could hear the loud thuds with each blow. Tufts of hair went flying. Then, both animals began to tire, and Wybl turned and ran. DCH chased him close and hard, down the hill, over a knoll and out of sight. In a few minutes DCH returned and rejoined his female.

Another much more dramatic and unusual fight was between White-horn and V5. Clashing horns and buffeting each other, they proceeded downhill and into a patch of forest. For a while I kept track of them by the quivering bushes and the sound of breaking branches. Then, following them into the forest, I was amazed to find V5 peering into a hole in the ground. White-horn had evidently fallen into the hole, and was now being pushed back in every time he tried to emerge.

V5 continued his attacks for three hours. During all the stamping and digging up of soil, the rim of the hole caved in and formed a ramp down to White-horn. But several large roots prevented him from getting out without laying himself open to serious head-banging. V5's final act, before departure, was to jam White-horn further in by pushing and pummeling with all his might. Apparently satisfied with his day's work, he went back to his group.

I returned the next morning to find White-horn still inside the earth cave. I thought he was dead, but felt a deep breath as I hooked my arm around him and tried to pull him out. He was alive, and trapped in the small cavity: a ridiculous, underground tahr. Normally I am inclined to let nature take its course, but this was a strange and exceptional case, so I broke a branch from a nearby tree and began to dig. After about an hour I was able to turn White-horn around so he was facing the entrance, lying on his side. I waited, and the only sign of life was an occasional flick of the ears. An hour later he shifted onto his chest and rested until I left three hours later. When I visited his cave that afternoon, he was standing beside it, but I have never seen a more miserable looking animal. He was covered with mud from head to tail; one eye was swollen shut. The next morning, he was gone and his tracks headed down through the forest. I never saw him again.

That was the last fight I saw. The rut was almost over and so was my study. The monsoon rains were finally easing, though the streams still ran in spate and the waterfalls still roared. I was thankful to be able to hike those beautiful hills without a hood over my head, and feel the warm sunshine on my shoulders. I was making plans to leave, but I was worried about leaving the tame tahr, *my* tahr as I now thought of them. Would they be all right? How long would it take them to regain their original and necessary fear of man? How many would the poachers get before the tahr got the message?

I brought some firecrackers back with me from a nearby town, thinking I might be able to teach them to be afraid of humans again. On the blustery day of my departure, I found them grazing peacefully on a grassy ridge. Running towards them I waved my arms and shouted, but they only ran in a tight circle and stood looking at me, puzzled. I lit a firecracker and threw it in their direction. The bang startled them a bit, but no more than a clap of thunder. There was nothing more I could do but hope for the best, so I turned and ran down the hill.

Postscript: I had the chance to return to Eavikulam for two days in September of 2006, twenty-five years after my study.

My hike up to Eravikulam was similar to my very first one, a jolly battle with the elements. I didn't see a single tahr, but I did see the insides of clouds and a lot of water—water in the streams, water on the grass, and water flying at me from the clouds. On the second day the clouds still streamed in from the west, but broke up and let the sun shine on my old stomping grounds. Whatever had happened immediately after I left, the tahr were fully wild again, and I had to seek cover and use the terrain to avoid making them run off. They are still there eight generations later, going about their business, and I hope it is forever so.

Tiger Cave

Ashish Chandola

Every forest has its mysterious and wonderful nooks and crannies. These only reveal themselves to the careful, silent, respectful visitor. One of these magical places is Ram Tallaiya in Madhya Pradesh. It has a forest pool so clear that in the shade of the tall Terminalia trees its waters appear a deep turquoise. Some such forest nooks include remnants of human settlements lost in the fog of time: like the ruins that one chances upon in the jungles of Sri Lanka and south India. Suddenly, one sees a hero-stone strangled by vines and creepers, or an old pillar overgrown with weeds. What could it have been, once upon a time? Then there are the animal-made structures like the tall termite mounds, or strange forms gouged out from salt-laden earth by elephants and rhinos.

Filming and photographing wildlife is a heady cocktail of challenge, frustration and reward. The rewards make up for the frustrating moments . . . such as when I saw and photographed a tiger drinking at one of the huge ancient water tanks at Bandhavgarh Fort. Waiting for rhinos at the edge of a small bheel or lake at Kaziranga, I couldn't believe my eyes when rhino after rhino emerged from the tall grass. There were twenty-two altogether, old and young, male and female, mothers and calves, all wallowing together under the mid-day sun.

I have always been happiest working from a well-positioned hide. Though hours spent on constant watch can be very tiring, hide work causes little disturbance to wildlife. However, it has its difficult moments, like the time a small snake insisted on getting under the cushion I was sitting on. Sometimes your body rebels against the hours of statue-like stillness. Once, I was filming jacanas from a hide over a swamp. An added bonus was a mugger crocodile, which was keeping a close watch on me. But then, cramps demanded moving around a bit, and the croc slowly sank into the murky waters and disappeared. A more unusual problem was when a three toed kingfisher decided to make the hide its perch, making my task impossible! Yes, it's nice to get close to wildlife . . . but too close isn't helpful either.

*

Dry heat, with temperatures touching 45 degrees C in the shade, is the hallmark of the summer months in central India. Mid-March is already hot in Bandhavgarh National Park (now a tiger reserve) in Madhya Pradesh, and by early April temperatures reach 40 degrees C by eight-thirty in the morning.

I knew this as I set off to film tigers at Bandhavgarh. It is well known that tigers hate the heat and will find cool spots in the forest to lie in during the hottest part of the day.

So do the langur monkeys and chital deer. Sambar, the largest of the ungulates found at Bandhavgarh, stop grazing in the swamps and head for the cover of the forested hills. Here, they spend most of the day in deep shade, browsing on the leaves of shrubs and bushes or just sitting around. Unlike humans, animals are sensible and don't feel guilty about doing nothing.

By 8.30 a.m., even birds stop calling with the exception of the 'coppersmith' barbet that somehow finds the energy to keep going: *tonk tonk tonk*. Its call is only punctuated by the harsh screeches of the tree pie.

We had been filming tigers during the winter months and things were going pretty well. Pugmarks left on dusty forest roads and paths enabled us to locate and keep up with the eight tigers we'd come to recognize and know. The Forest Department had provided me with a young tusker elephant named Bandhav Gaj and his mahout Phool Singh. Every day we followed tiger tracks on paths made through the grasslands by chital, wild boar and other wildlife.

Tigers prefer using such 'beaten' paths as it is much easier than making new ones through the tangle of grass and bushes that form the forest floor. And it was along these forest trails that Phool Singh and I, perched on Bandhav Gaj, would follow one of the known tigers. When we spotted a tiger, or a tigress with cubs, my task was to film and photograph them as unobtrusively as possible.

There were times when the alarm calls of deer and monkeys alerted us to the presence and movement of a tiger.

The light in the winter months is crisp and golden, wonderful for photography and filming. With the progression of the seasons, this changes. At Bandhavgarh, very suddenly one day the light loses this glow and we know that the summer months are upon us.

The advent of summer created a major problem for Phool Singh and his tusker. With the increasing heat of the day, the forest paths became hard and dusty, and the wet patches on which tiger pugmarks would be imprinted vanished.

After days of fruitless searching for tiger signs, Phool Singh suggested we give Bandhav Gaj a rest, take to our feet, and check out the rocky outcrops that dot the Bandhavgarh landscape. Surely, these would still hold some pools of water, however small, which the tigers could be using to cool off during the day.

And sure enough, we did come across water . . . but in tiny puddles covered with fallen leaves and swarming with bees. There were no large pools, and no signs of tigers. But giving up isn't an option in wildlife photography. We searched day after day and then quite unexpectedly, one afternoon, stumbled across one of those magical places that people like me dream about.

It was a cave, large but not very deep, and heavily shaded by a majestic stand of tall sal trees. It rose steeply to over twenty feet at one end and tapered down to the ground at the other. Its floor, covered with sand, was cool and wet from the water of a natural spring underneath. And I must say I have never seen so many tiger tracks in one place. Several males, and a female with cubs! We wasted no time and built a hide at the tapered end of the cave, using stones and boulders just big enough to accommodate the camera, tripod and me.

We were at the secret tiger cave by six the next morning. Phool Singh helped me set up the camera, wished me luck, and left. He would return at five in the evening to pick me up. I began my tiger vigil.

Though small, my hide was comfortable enough. It was also quite cool and very dark. To add to this, there was a constant breeze that flowed in my direction from the far end. This made me confident that tigers approaching the shelter would not be able to smell me.

I had barely settled down in my 'home' for the day, when the deep 'dhank dhank' alarm call of a sambar put me on full alert. Almost immediately, I saw a tiger clambering over the large rocks at the opposite end. It was approaching the shelter. With the camera singing in my ear (yes it does when you have your ear to it, but no one else can hear it!) I could see through the viewfinder that it was a tigress. Then, as my heart missed a beat or two, three cubs appeared, one after another.

They walked into the deep shade of the cave and settled down in its coolness. I had a close-up, fascinating view of the little interactions that took place—cubs moving around and changing places, the tigress grooming and licking them, little tiger-cub sounds of pleasure and irritation. And suddenly, out of nowhere, to my utter surprise there was a huge male tiger amongst them! The camera viewfinder had restricted my vision, and I hadn't seen him approaching.

The large male stood on the wet sand and licked his side before moving forward to flop down, pushing one of the cubs aside in the process. Slowly he stretched his powerful fore-quarters to the full and made himself comfortable. At this point, the underside of one huge paw was facing the camera, and his chin pointed skywards in an utterly relaxed pose.

I had five tigers sleeping, resting and socializing only yards away from me, totally oblivious of my presence. It was only nine-thrity in the morning and a fascinating tiger day stretched ahead.

By three in the afternoon the tigers began to stir, and soon left the shelter. By the time Bandhav Gaj arrived to pick me up, they had vanished into their forest home leaving only their footprints in the sand of the cave and a deeply elated photographer. I could hardly believe that I had shared a cave with five tigers for close to ten hours!

After spending a few more days with the tigers in the cave, Phool Singh and I dismantled the hide and scattered the stones and boulders back to their original places. The brief human presence was gone. The tigers were on their own once more.

Ralph Morris of the Biligiris

Monica Jackson

The first foreigner to visit the Biligirirangan Hills near Mysore was my paternal grandfather, Randolph Morris. There were local stories about another, earlier British 'dorai' (sahib), possibly a government surveyor. But he sounded more mythical than real, the stories about him more colourful than plausible. Apparently he rode up on an elephant, scattering silver coins along the way. Europeans, being white and spooky-looking, often got entangled in local myth and legend in those days.

Randolph, who came from Perthshire in Scotland, was a coffee planter in Coorg and then in the Nilgiri hills. The

Biligiri range is visible from the northern slopes of the Nilgiris. Intrigued by what was then unknown territory, he decided to explore that rugged wilderness. In 1885, he arrived there on horseback and discovered what bordered on paradise in his eyes: an area of great natural beauty, with unlimited wildlife and good conditions for growing coffee. He decided to settle there.

In 1888, he established and planted Attikan, the first of four coffee estates our family owned. This was done under extremely difficult conditions, such as the herds of understandably resentful elephants. Randolph died in 1918 after being gored by a bull bison. He is buried on a hilltop in the range, where his grave is carefully tended to this day. Incidentally my mother's father, an authority on wildlife, was also killed by a wild animal: in his case, a wild boar.

The last and largest of the estates, Honnametti, belonged to his son, Ralph Morris, who became something of a legend among the local people for his courage, generosity and knowledge of the jungle. Stories about him still circulate among the present generation of the Sholiga tribe in his beloved Biligiris. His articles and observations have been published in the journal of the Bombay Natural History Society and other publications, and are still read and quoted. Like Jim Corbett, he started off as a hunter but later 'converted' to conservation. And, last but not least, he was my father.

Our home in Honnametti was perched on a hill overlooking slopes of coffee bushes and the jungle-clad foothills to the east of the range. The house was long and ranch-like, rather ordinary from the outside but full of charm and comfort inside. The beautiful gardens tapered off into the rainforest. Gardening was only one of Mummy's skills: she also ran a small dairy, poultry, and vegetable and fruit gardens. She was the most capable mechanic on the estate, and its doctor and nurse. My father Ralph often left estate matters in her hands, and spent most of his time in the jungle with his friends the Sholigas, a tribe famous for its knowledge of the forest and its wildlife. Being a good hunter, he was also often called upon to shoot a rogue elephant or cattle-marauding tiger.

When I revisited the hills years later, I met an old Sholiga who had been one of my father's favourite companions. I asked after his health, and he replied: 'I am waiting to die. I am waiting for your father to call me from the next world and then we shall be together again.'

What was it like to grow up in Honnametti? Needless to say, it was a privileged life. My sister Sheila and I had all the liberty and space we could use. For our endless secret games, we had the freedom of acres of garden and the adjoining woodlands. Our friends and confidants were the house and garden staff, above all the boys employed to look after the dogs and herd the cows. Sheila tended to fall in love with the cow-boys, but I loved Mada, the dog-boy, who climbed trees with us and corrected our ungrammatical Kannada.

Our other companions were the dogs, the cows, the chickens and our ponies. Sheila had a little black cart bull who drew us in a miniature cart. My special animal was a black Labrador of a highly individual and eccentric personality.

Instead of having to go to school, we were taught by our mother's sister, who lived with us in our early years. We had many wonderful books to read. Above all, we were surrounded by the jungle and its denizens. Ralph took us on adventurous camping trips and showed us tigers, panthers, bears, wild dogs, wild pigs, sambar and chital. We sat up in observation machans over waterholes on moonlit nights to watch elephants splashing in the pools. We saw herds of bison grazing alongside our own cattle. We went into the jungle with the Sholigas, who gave us wild honey, fruit and fungi to eat. And we competed with each other about the number of leech bites we collected during the monsoons.

Ralph was, like most of the human species, a many-sided character. As children we loved him because he was funny, and also (I regret to say) because of his irresponsibility, which made him a better playmate than most grown-ups. And irresponsible he was, sometimes risking our lives to satisfy his perennial curiosity about the workings of nature. For instance, we were once driving through scrub jungle at the foot of our hills. My parents were in the car, Ralph at the wheel, and my sister Sheila and I sitting on the wings outside. Turning a corner, we came upon two panthers sunbathing in the middle of the track. Ralph stopped, and we and the panthers regarded each other in silence. Then the panthers moved to the side of the track, still staring uneasily. Sheila and I were enthralled, and so was Ralph, who leaned out of the window and whistled, to see what would happen. Our mother, anxious because her children were sitting unprotected within a few feet of the big felines, whispered 'Drive on, Ralph'. He appeared not to hear, and whistled again. By this time the panthers were twitching their tails and growling, and Mummy leaned over, grabbed the wheel and yelled at him, 'Drive on at once.' He did so, slowly and reluctantly.

When I was about sixteen, he took me on a tiger beat. A pair of tigers had been terrorizing a village and preying on their cattle, so the villagers asked for Ralph's help. He organized a band of beaters, wielding rattles and drums, to move into a nullah in which the tigers had been lying up, while he and I walked ahead, along one side of the nullah. After a while, we heard a roar from one of the tigers. They were understandably reluctant to leave their siesta in the heat of the day and be driven uphill by a noisy mob.

Eventually, when the beaters were drawing level with us, we heard a series of shattering roars from the tigers and frightened yells from the villagers. Ralph stopped. 'They need me in the nullah, the tigers are trying to break back,' he said. 'I must protect the beaters.' He looked at me speculatively and picked up a handful of small stones from the hard ground. 'If a tiger comes up here, throw these at it.' Then he was off, rifle on shoulder, down into the nullah.

I wasn't too happy about the situation: an unarmed sixteen-year-old girl sitting on the ground in the path of an angry tiger. I decided I was not going to further enrage it by chucking pebbles at it. There were some scrawny saplings around, but they looked frail and insecure. As the first of the beaters reached me, a tiger bounded out of the nullah with a final thunderous roar and the men shinnied up all the available trees. There was nothing I could do but sit and admire the tiger, which was indeed so beautiful that I forgot to be frightened. It galloped past us and we heard a rifle shot, as my father tried to turn the other tiger.

Well, both the tigers got away, I'm glad to say. But, unsettled by the day's events, they decided to depart from that valley to seek their fortunes elsewhere and the villagers were left in peace. So the story ended happily for all concerned.

Another time Ralph was called upon by distraught villagers to rid them of a very nasty man-killing rogue elephant. Along with my mother, two visiting friends, my sister and me, he set off to the village concerned to identify the animal.

We camped near the village that night, and in the morning, village graziers having pinpointed the elephant's whereabouts, we all set off through the hot, dusty, undulating bamboo jungle. Eventually we reached the top of a small hill, below which was a steep little valley where the elephant was feeding. We had been watching it for a while when it suddenly shifted and lifted its trunk. 'The wind has changed,' Ralph whispered. 'We should go.' Which we did hastily, trying to move quietly, though since we were a party of six local men and six Brits in a bamboo forest where every step crackled, this proved impossible.

Darkness came on, and we stopped in a clearing for the villagers to make brushwood torches and light them. As they did so, my father heard a stick crack in the thicket behind us. 'Look out,' he warned, 'the rogue's here.' And out into the clearing it surged, its trunk up, ready to charge. Ralph and the two visitors, who were also armed, swung rifles to shoulders. The villagers, Mummy, Sheila and I took doubtful refuge beneath a few small thorny trees in the vicinity. As the rogue reached us, three rifles fired, the bullets making fiery streaks in the darkness. The elephant fell within a metre of us.

What was so amazing was that the huge animal had stalked us so silently. It was fortunate for us all that Ralph's jungle experience and instinct had ensured that his ears were pricked for signals of what he suspected might happen.

Other adventures with my father included the time when a bear pursued us so doggedly that it climbed the rocks of a steep outcrop to get at us; and also the time when I was eight and Ralph, following two bears through long grass to discover their cave, forgot I was with him. He left me, lost and disconsolate, in grass taller than I was. My relief was huge when a Sholiga appeared. '*Aiyo, kusu* (child),' he said, and scooped me up and carried me down to where Ralph was happily peering into a complex of rocks and caves. About fifty years later I was visiting the Biligiri Hills as an anthropologist and met Sholiga Jeddia again. 'I know that face,' I exclaimed. 'And so you should,' he replied with a broad grin, 'since I carried you in my arms.'

Once, again in the vicinity of a rogue elephant, Ralph disappeared in search of it, leaving my sister and I with a Sholiga in a shola (patch of evergreen forest). After a while we heard an ominous *thud, thud, thud*. It was the elephant approaching. We all began eyeing the surrounding trees in the hope of climbing them, when Ralph appeared as if from nowhere. 'Rogue's coming,' he whispered unnecessarily. 'Hurry up.' Needless to say, we did.

These are just a few of the adventures with which our father enlivened our childhood. Being with him in the wilderness was always interesting, often exciting, sometimes frightening. I wouldn't have missed it for anything, and it led me to seek adventure in its various aspects for the rest of my life. But Honnametti meant more to us than adventures with elephants and tigers. When my parents decided to leave their beloved Biligiris in the 1950s and return to England, it was an enormous loss for Sheila and me. In losing Honnametti, we lost our roots. Being young and flexible, we managed; though that sense of nostalgia never went away. But Ralph was heartbroken and never the same again. He had left his heart in the jungles of his beloved mountain range and with it his sense of identity and purpose.

M. Krishnan: Nature's Spokesman

Ramachandra Guha

My wife and I were recently discussing people we admired. High on her list was the artist and writer Manjula Padmanabhan. And high on mine, in fact on top of it, was M. Krishnan (1912–96), likewise an artist and writer of varied gifts and originality of expression.

Krishnan was, among other things, an accomplished writer in Tamil. He grew up in Mylapore in Chennai, the youngest son of the celebrated novelist and social reformer A. Madhaviah. Krishnan's own last work was a detective novel in his mother tongue. A posthumous collection of his Tamil essays, edited by the scholar and naturalist Theodore

Baskaran, has been published under the title *Mazhaikkalamum Kuyilosaiyum*.

But he was also a very talented wildlife photographer. The camera he used was called (by himself and his acolytes) 'Super-Ponderosa'. It was put together from pieces garnered from here and there—a lens from East Germany, a cap and shutter from Malaysia, nuts and bolts from Burma Bazaar, the lot held together by some neighbourhood string. But it, and he, took staggeringly good pictures. Some are represented in a 1985 collection called *Nights and Days*; others, better still, in a book put together in 2006 by Ashish and Shanthi Chandola and T. N. A. Perumal, carrying the title *Eye in the Jungle*.

Then again, Krishnan was a marvellous prose stylist in his adopted language, English. Growing up, I spent many enjoyable hours in his company, reading his fortnightly 'Country Notebook' column in *The Statesman*. Much later, I had the privilege of making a selection from essays he had published over fifty years. This book was published in 2000; it is called *Nature's Spokesman: M. Krishnan and Indian Wildlife*.

Lastly, Krishnan was a pioneering environmentalist and conservationist. He knew and practised 'environmental education' before that term had been coined. Consider his essay 'Nature Study', printed in *The Hindu* on 18 May 1947. 'The school approach to nature study,' wrote this former schoolteacher, 'is fundamentally unsound. It is based on the theory that one must proceed from elementary, understandable things. There is simplification and selection, and logical, reasoned steps guide the approach. But the fact is that nature is not simple, logical and reasoned—thank God that it is not. There is no need to fully understand anything in all its structure and complexity to be alive to its charm . . . What makes living things fascinating is their behaviour, not their anatomy. Children in primary schools should get to know the common wild plants and birds of the locality; birds because they are so easily watched. They should learn, a little later perhaps, the stories of the domestic animals. They should be taken out to see nature for themselves, and be given pleasant books, with gay, colourful illustrations . . . Children love them, and will readily interest themselves in any text if it is free from morals and illustrated in colour.'

Krishnan was India's best *all-round* naturalist. Salim Ali knew more, much more, than him about Indian birds. Jim Corbett better understood the behaviour of large mammals in the wild. Some botanists were more closely acquainted with Indian plants, some herpetologists with Indian reptiles. But no one knew as much as Krishnan about so many different aspects of the natural world in India.

Krishnan lived and died in Chennai (known in his time as Madras), but spent much of the year in the field, accompanied only by his camera, a notebook, a sketch-pad, and a change of clothes. He was familiar with the snows of the Himalaya, the deserts of Rajasthan, the mangroves of the Sunderbans, and the grasslands of the Deccan. He wrote quite beautifully about these varied terrains, and about the insects, plants, birds and animals that inhabited them.

The best introduction to Krishnan is through his writings. So let me now quote from some of the thousands of nature essays that he published in his long and very full life. I shall begin with an essay published in 1961, when the government of India was deciding upon the choice of the National Bird. Here, Krishnan said the leading candidate was the peacock, for 'everyone knows it and has seen it, it is to be found all over India, and it is intimately and anciently associated with our religious and countryside legends and culture'. Further, 'it is so distinctive in its arresting beauty that it lends itself to unmistakable formalized description—in fact it has been so depicted in our folk and classical art.'

He went on to say, 'I shall be greatly surprised, why I shall be astonished if any other bird is ultimately preferred for the honour.' Still, to make the debate more interesting, he decided to 'press the claims of the Common Mynah'. These were his reasons: 'Though sacred to no god, it is well known to our legends and folksongs, and is one of the most familiar birds in the country, being especially common in and around human settlements, both in the plains and the lower hills. And in spite of being so common, few birds have a richer plumage as [the naturalist] Eha pointed out long ago. The contrast of the cadmium yellow of its legs and beak and facial patches with the Vandyke brown of its plumage and the black of its head and the blaze of white on each wing that lends its flight such vividness, are . . . contrasts that could be most effectively formalized in an emblem. It has an additional claim. It is frequently caged and trained to talk and in our folksongs it is often entrusted with the delivery of messages to loved ones far away, a kind of ambassadorial responsibility that is surely an asset in any National Bird.'

This passage carries the hallmarks of Krishnan's writing: an attention to the everyday aspects of Nature (not merely to its most spectacular forms or manifestations), an understanding of shape and size and colour and form (natural in a trained artist), a knowledge of our folk and literary traditions, and a sense of humour. These trademarks are also present in my next excerpt, from an essay on a resident of his own house, a lizard he had named (for reasons that he does not share with us) 'Lenin'. Of this creature Krishnan writes (in an essay published as early as 1938):

'Lenin has been there ever since I can remember. Once, long ago, he was small and lithe, and moved with a swift, easy grace. His tail would twist nervously from side to side, specially when some insect was near, for Lenin was eager and excitable in those days. His body would shine a warm, translucent orange in the glare of the wall-lamp, as your fingers would if you closed them over the bulb of a powerful electric torch. At times he was almost beautiful.

'All that is gone. Tonight (for he comes out only at night) he is fat and repulsive. His tail is thick and rigid, with a kink at the end of it, and he is no longer translucent. I never liked Lenin, but in the old days I used to admire his sinuous speed as he raced about the walls on his career of rapine and murder. Now he has no saving grace: he is just six inches of squat, warty ugliness.'

Here, next, are some observations made while spending time in Madras's famous Chepauk cricket ground:

'Watching India's first historic Test victory over England [in January 1952], along with a huge holiday crowd, were a dozen kites. They had followed the game with unrelaxing eyes over the previous three days, and I knew some of them by the close of the opening day.

'One had two forward primaries missing from each wing, one had a squarish tail, one was exceptionally light in colour, a bleached golden brown, another was almost black in its swarthy new plumage, and there was a bird that had lost the entire tail quite recently. I was amused by the vigilance of these birds, patrolling the sky above the ground. Whenever drinks were brought out to the players, the air overhead was suddenly thick with kites, swooping and circling low for a minute before sailing away disappointed. During the breaks for lunch and tea there were opportunist scrambles, some birds alighting on the grass to consume scraps thrown aside by the crowd, others flying away with the booty. Quite a few of the spectators, discussing the happenings and prospects excitedly, had the hurried morsel expertly plucked from their hands. Especially was I amused by a sandwich-eater who laughed uproariously at his neighbour's loss, only to have his own bread snatched the next moment—the sheepish smile on his face was worth going a long way to see.'

From encounters in the home or the city let us move on to an encounter in the wild. An essay of 1959 begins with these vivid paragraphs:

'There was a regular wall of screw-pine, ten feet high and grown in a thick tangle, bordering the shallow streamlet on either side, and as we approached a gap in it some heavy animal rose from the nullah and crashed its way through the farther wall of screw-pine. From the sounds of its passage, we knew that it was something really large and massive, and for a moment my mahout turned as near grey as his dark complexion would allow.

'"Onti!" he whispered.

'There was a singularly aggressive lone tusker in that area, whose movements we had to study each day in order to avoid a possible brush with him in the jungles, and that morning we had taken the usual precautions. "Onti" in Kannada means "singleton", i. e., a lone bull—and knowing the likely reactions of this notorious tusker to men on elephant-back, we had every reason to feel apprehensive, but a second later we could see for ourselves that it was no tusker that we had flushed from the cool retreat of that fenced-in watercourse. It was a gaunt old gaur bull, black as night and huge, with thick, blunt horns that swept out in a wide curve—the lack of fodder of dry March was reflected in the way his great ribs stood out on his sides.'

One feature of Krishnan's life and work was his deep identification with the Indian landscape. Krishnan was an ecological patriot, who believed that the essence of Indianness lay in the species and habitats distinctive to the land. When, in the first flush of Independence, the nation was restless to build—to build dams, steel mills, atomic plants and the like—Krishnan warned (in an essay published in *The Hindu* in December 1958) that 'we are a very ancient nation too, and there are vital matters in which we need to be conservative rather than constructive'. He complained that 'particularly we are given to the introduction of exotic plants in our desire to beautify the countryside and make up by plantation for the annihilation of jungle and woodland that we have been responsible for during the past fifty years . . . No country in the world has a flora so rich in exotics as India'. He recommended that we cultivate 'a narrow sort of patriotism in our floral preferences'. In other words, to be truly Indian, one must plant (and protect) Indian.

All his life, Krishnan underlined the connections between conservation and nationhood. An essay of 1974, printed in the *Times of India Annual*, put it this way: 'If we are wise, we can save India and her magnificent heritage of nature for the generations of Indians to come, and safeguard the physical and organic integrity of our country, threatened today—we can give them a country to be truly proud of. Will we?' Twenty-two years later, in a column published in *The Statesman* on the day he died, Krishnan suggested that the snag 'seems to lie in our Constitution, evolved by men with formidable knowledge of legal and political matters and hardly any of the unique biotic richness of India—they do not even seem to have realized that the identity of a country depended not so much on its mutable human culture as on its geomorphology, flora and fauna, its *natural* basis.'

On the Trail of the Giant Crocs

Rom Whitaker

A Real Twenty-footer

It all started way back in 1980 when I was on patrol with my friend Jerome Montague on the Fly River in a remote corner of Papua New Guinea. We were cruising along in our twenty-foot long flat-bottomed boat when we were flagged down by a group of excited villagers at Komovai, not far from the river mouth. They had just hauled in a fishing net and its contents had left their jaws hanging open—it was a huge saltwater crocodile. Seriously huge. The villagers had skinned the croc and when we put a tape on it, the measurement came to 6.21 metres, a little over twenty feet!

There are lots of stories of twenty- and even thirty-foot crocs; but without a skin, skull, good photographs or other hard evidence they remain mere fables. That twenty-foot skin we measured still remains the biggest on record with the evidence to back it up. My question was, do such monster size crocs still exist or has the 'giant gene' been wiped out by hunters who always go for the biggest animals? Also, giant crocs aren't very popular or cuddly . . . and there are precious few places remote enough where a potentially dangerous animal can live in peace and grow to a huge size.

My quest to find giant crocodiles became a bit of an obsession and I started gathering whatever data I could on croc measurements. Being part of the Crocodile Specialist Group of the International Union for the Conservation of Nature meant that I could tap into a vast network of good croc people around the world for facts and figures on giant crocs. I got skull measurements and pictures from all over and started to sift through the evidence. The first question was, which of the twenty-three species of crocs in the world had the potential to reach a length of twenty feet . . . and where are they still found? The available data narrowed the search down to six species:

Saltwater crocodile: Found from India through to Australia

Nile crocodile: Found throughout much of Africa and Madagascar

American crocodile: Now rare but still found in Florida and parts of South America

Orinoco crocodile: Found in northern South America

False gharial: A very rare species, now found only on Borneo and the Malay peninsula

Gharial: Another very rare species restricted to North India and Nepal

Big Skulls

One of the most exciting finds was right here in India where the skull of a monster saltwater croc (salty for short) resides with my friend Prince Shivendra, the erstwhile Maharaja of Kanika in coastal Orissa. The croc was called Kalia, and when it was alive in the 1930s, was reputedly a ladies' man; most of the twenty people it had eaten were women. It was finally shot, and supposedly measured twenty-three feet in length. The skull measures 73.3 centimetres, just under thirty inches. Croc experts had long used a ratio of skull length multiplied by 7 to calculate the total length of salties, but using this formula Kalia would have only been seventeen and a half feet long. When we measured the head length and total length of our own Jaws III, a good sized salty at the Madras Crocodile Bank, the ratio was closer to 1:9. Using this ratio Kalia becomes about twenty-two and a half feet long, much closer to the original story.

Other skull lengths came zipping in by email, and my croc chart soon overflowed with numbers. The biggest skull was 76 centimetres, from a salty killed long ago in Cambodia which now resides in the Paris museum. According to our 1:9 ratio, this guy would have been close to twenty-three feet long.

But there are much bigger skulls around. There are skulls over 80 centimetres (thirty-two inches) long of gharial and false gharial, long-snouted fish-eaters which are definite candidates for the 'over twenty feet' category. But we know very little about the skull length to total length ratio of these species, which just complicated my job even further!

Expedition Giant Crocs

Having done all this homework with skulls, pictures and old hunters' stories, it was now time to get out there and find some of those huge crocs. But how and where should I begin? The answer came in the form of a filmmaker friend from England, who called to ask if I was interested in presenting a film on giant crocs. This was perfect! They were paying me to fly all over the world to try to find monster crocs; a dream come true.

To cut a long story short, I was soon winging my way across the world to Florida to meet some large captive crocs and alligators and to talk to colleagues about where to look. It became evident that the three likeliest places to find that monster croc were Africa, India and Australia (well, New Guinea too, but I had to make do with three spots).

So, after a few quick measurements of some zoo crocs and 'gators in Florida, the next stop was Australia.

Australian Outback

We chartered a small plane to fly us from Darwin, way up in the Northern Territory, to the Bullo River Cattle Station, a million-acre ranch with a prime croc river flowing through it. We were there because a monster croc had been spotted several times, and judging from its tracks it measured well over twenty feet. We spent several days flying sorties over the river by helicopter, having a great time and now and then diving down for a closer look at some of the larger salties that lay basking on the wide mud banks. On the third day we spotted what looked like a really good-sized salty and swept in for a closer look. Our approach startled the croc and the big heavy fellow lifted himself clear off the mud bank and dived into the deep channel. What amazed us was that he left behind an absolutely perfect impression of himself in the mud; you could even count the scales on his tail. This was a good chance for a measurement, so the chopper let me off onto the mud and I took a quick measurement: sixteen feet two inches; big, but no giant.

During the week we were at Bullo, we saw some hefty crocs and eventually found a track of one which could easily have been the Bullo River monster croc, but we never saw him.

Salties of Bhitarkanika

The next leg of our trip was back in India to try and track down those gigantic salties that supposedly live in the Bhitarkanika

Sanctuary in coastal Orissa. In fact, the Guinness Book of Records states that this is where the biggest crocs in the world live, including a record size twenty-three-footer. I'm not sure if history was getting confused with reality here, and it's too bad there just wasn't enough time to prove or disprove the claim of the biggest in the world. The weather had already turned a bit warm and crocs weren't too interested in basking, limiting the number of big crocs we could see. We did a couple of night rides on the boat and counted over seventy-five crocs in a few hours, which was gratifying, but no behemoths turned up. During the boat trips, we saw some huge tracks (eighteen-footers I would guess) and a couple of cruising crocs that were huge, but not the record size ones we sought. Interestingly, an alleged nineteen-foot salty that had been found dead in the river was buried right where we were staying in Dangmal. The Forest Department very graciously allowed us to dig up the skeleton which did look big, but after putting all the bones together it didn't top seventeen feet. Reluctantly we left Bhitarkanika and I vowed to get back as soon as I could to try to confirm the existence of the biggest crocs in the world.

Gharial—the Crocodile from Mars

Heading north, we arrived at a beautiful spot just next to the Nepal border, Katerniaghat Wildlife Sanctuary. Fifteen kilometres of the Girwa River flows through the sanctuary, and this is the second most important place for the survival of the critically endangered gharial. There were definitely some twenty-foot candidates here and we decided we must try to measure the big males of this strangest of all the crocs. And here's how we did it: The assistant cameraman was also a computer whiz and figured out how to get an accurate measurement of a gharial basking on the bank without having to catch it. We had a pair of sophisticated, range-finding binoculars (apparently used by the military to target and blow things out of existence) and we'd find a basking animal as close to perpendicular as possible and get its exact distance from us. Then we'd take a picture of the beast from that spot using a fixed focal length, in this case 200 mm. Putting the picture on to Photoshop (our man had his laptop right there next to the river) the pixel length of the gharial would be converted to millimetres.

This would be multiplied by the distance in millimetres and then divided by the focal length, giving a very accurate length of the beast. Just to cross-check, I went over to the sand bank and lay down in the same spot as the gharial (he moved off before I got there of course). Since I'm exactly six feet tall, it was easy to confirm the length of the gharial by comparing it to how many 'Rom lengths' appeared on the computer screen. But after patting ourselves on the back about this high-tech approach to remote croc measuring, we put it to our local guide Ram Roop: 'How long do you think that gharial is?' we asked smugly. He answered in a flash, 'I would think sixteen feet' . . . exactly what our range finder, camera and computer told us!

No twenty-foot gharial, but let's not forget that the

recovery of croc populations in most parts of the world has only been happening for twenty-five or thirty years, not long enough to produce the real giants of yesteryear. I was inclined to think that the giant genes probably still exist; the crocs just need time to grow to those huge sizes.

Nile Crocs of the Rift Valley

Next stop Africa, at beautiful Lake Chamo nestled in the Rift Valley of Ethiopia. The Nile crocodile has been protected here from skin hunters for three decades, and the population has made a dramatic recovery with close to 2,000 adult crocs. Our Cessna flew in low over the lake before settling down at the Arba Minch airport, and we spotted several nice big Niles basking in the morning sun. We visited the croc ranch there with its 5,000 young crocs being raised for skins and meat. They had a bunch of skulls of big Nile crocs that had drowned in fishing nets. Some that I measured are the largest on record in any museum and close to the size of the largest salty skulls we'd measured. This gave us some idea of what was awaiting us. We'd been told of the spot where the Kolfu River enters Lake Chamo, called the 'crocodile market' where crocs congregate to bask. And that's where we'd be heading next morning.

Lake Chamo is at 4,000 feet, and the morning had a slight chill till the sun burnt through the light mist. And that's when the crocs started climbing up on the banks to bask. The 'crocodile market' exceeded all our expectations. I counted 173 crocs in the first two hours, getting almost close enough to touch some of them—a tempting idea. Over the next few days we saw the biggest crocs of our entire trip. The Lake Chamo Nile ones are amongst the largest of all crocs left in the world—some we measured remotely were over eighteen feet long!

Finale

Well, we didn't find a twenty-footer, but the crocs and evidence of big ones we saw were enough to convince me that they are still out there. I wasn't at all disappointed; we'd found a few spots on the planet where big crocs are still allowed to survive and I now have an excuse to go on another trip around the world looking for that monster croc. Is anyone out there interested in sending me?

Into the Tiger's World

George Schaller

One evening I sat at the edge of a nullah in Kanha National Park. Below me were the remains of a cow killed by a tiger the previous night, and I waited for the cat's return. A single dry leaf rustled behind me. Cautiously I looked back over the boulder against which I had been leaning. A tigress stood ten feet away. Briefly I felt like running away but knew that I must remain calm and quiet. The tigress stared at me with amber eyes, then walked away, looking back once over her shoulder.

That incident occurred nearly half a century ago. I had come to central India with my wife, Kay, and two small sons to study tigers and the tiger's prey, such as wild pig, chital and sambar. Today much is known about the habits of tigers because of the dedicated research of Ullas Karanth, Valmik Thapar, Raghu Chundawat and others. But back in the early 1960s there were mainly hunters' tales.

I was eager to find out about the tiger's social life. How widely does a tiger travel? How do tigers communicate? How often does a tiger have to kill to survive? By answering these and many other questions, I hoped not only to learn about the tiger's life but also to help protect this beautiful cat. Good conservation can only be based on good knowledge. Remote Kanha in the highlands of Madhya Pradesh, with its sal forests and maidans where deer came to drink and graze, was perfect for my proposed study. The Forest Department provided us with a bungalow past which tigers wandered. Indeed, one hungry tiger clawed a hole into our bamboo shed and carried away a lamb we were saving for Christmas dinner.

It takes patience to study tigers. Most of the cats have learned that humans mean danger and they hide or vanish silently on velvet paws when detecting a person. I cruised forest roads in my vehicle, always hoping for at least a glimpse of tawny striped fur. But mostly I preferred to walk because I could see, smell, and hear so much better this way. Tigers often wandered roads, trails and along nullahs where I found their tracks (those of a big male tiger could be up to six inches in diameter). At places a cat would have raked its hind paws on the ground to create a bare spot or scrape, and at times it veered to a tree where cuts in the bark showed claw marks.

These must be sign posts, I concluded, at which the tiger advertised its presence by both marks and odour.

Even food habits can be determined without ever meeting a tiger. Faeces—or scats as field biologists call them—are often full of hair that has not been digested. I would pull them apart and note the length, colour and thickness of hair. Tigers preyed mostly on chital, sambar and gaur, but they also killed domestic cattle and buffalo, and sometimes they pounced on a langur that had come to the ground. Often I heard the shrill alarm calls of chital; they had sensed a predator. Was it tiger or merely leopard or jackal?

Naturally I wanted to observe tigers when they were not disturbed by my presence. During brief meetings, I had marvelled at their power, elegance and flaming beauty. With binoculars I was able to bring them closer and look into their faces, where I noticed that the black stripes and markings, were as distinctive as a fingerprint. This enabled me to identify individuals, and with time I learned that one male and three females lived near our home within an area of about 25 square miles. Several others visited but did not stay. Sometimes when a tiger met me inadvertently on a forest trail, it flattened its ears and snarled with gleaming two-inch canines to intimidate me. This gave me time to check the markings on its face. To meet a 450-pound male tiger in this manner can greatly concentrate the mind . . .

The best way to observe tigers at leisure was to find them on a kill. A tiger may remain for several days with the body of a sambar or other large prey, eating, sleeping, and eating some more. Vultures and crows often crowd into a tree above a kill, waiting for scraps, and their noisy presence alerted me. I would then find a nearby tree and settle motionless on to a branch with a view of the kill. Sometimes I sat there all night, the wind rustling the leaves, alone except for the tiger who had returned to its meal. When the moon comes up, a tiger seems to float through the still night like a silver shadow. Far away another tiger may call, a hollow and resonant roar: *aauuu, aa-uuu*, a sound that electrified the forest. 'Here I am,' the tiger proclaims, demanding awe and respect. Even though you feel cramped and stiff and tired, you dare not sleep. A sudden movement or fall might disturb the animal at its kill. One night I was in a low, gnarled tree listening to a tigress with four large cubs on a kill in the darkness of a nullah. There were growls and the grating of tooth on bone. Because of a tattered ear, I had named this tigress Cut-ear (though I should have used a more evocative name such as Sundari, 'Beautiful', for this lovely animal). Suddenly my body seemed aflame: an army of ants had climbed the tree by the hundred and bitten me. I leaped out of the tree and ran into the night. The tigers became silent, listening to my noisy departure. They can be tolerant animals.

Such nightly vigils gave me unique insights into the tiger's social life. It had been thought that tigers were strictly solitary, avoiding each other except for a mother with cubs. Males were considered brutes who killed cubs. But consider observations such as these: Cut-ear called loudly, *aa-uuu*, after she made a kill, apparently to notify her cubs. Soon they came. Did they recognize her voice? From afar another tiger also answered Cut-ear's call, and over an hour later yet another tigress with one cub arrived. A total of seven tigers now shared a kill. The male tiger was an amiable chap with a scraggly ruff. Once when Cut-ear and her cubs were at a kill, he suddenly appeared. Although he was hungry, his belly lean, he waited patiently until everyone had finished before taking a bite. The cubs rubbed their faces against his in greeting. He remained with the family until morning before resuming his rounds—solitary but not unsociable.

Cut-ear also taught me about life in a tiger family. Cubs are born blind and helpless and they weigh a mere two to three pounds. At eight weeks of age, they are able to move with their mother, and at six months, when the size of a large dog, they are weaned. To feed her hungry brood of two to three and even four, a tigress has to hunt relentlessly. Prey is alert and most stalks end in failure. Cut-ear herself needed at least fifteen pounds of meat a day. When she killed a chital, she and her cubs finished all but some bones and stomach content within hours. Once I met her as she dragged a freshly killed gaur calf into a nullah. She then left to fetch her cubs. While she was gone, I weighed the carcass. At dusk all returned to the feast. In the morning when the family left to rest by a water hole, I again weighed the gaur remains. The family had eaten 85 pounds of meat.

At eight to ten months of age, the cubs occasionally followed their mother on a hunt, but only as spectators. Even when one year old, they had little experience in the art of killing. Once I observed as the tigress felled a buffalo without injuring it and she then watched as her three female cubs bit and clawed without grabbing the throat in a stranglehold, which is the proper way to kill. She had given them the chance to learn.

Cut-ear's male cub, larger than his sisters, had left them to go on his own and become a nuisance in his quest for food. He entered the village and grabbed a pig, and another time he demolished a chicken house to get at the five occupants. However, he maintained contact with his family and conveniently showed up whenever there was something to eat. By the age of two years, all of the cubs would be independent.

So step by step, over many months, I gained some insights into the tiger's world. To kill to live is the tiger's main concern. The species requires so little to survive: natural prey, some shade, water, and freedom from persecution. Yet its fate now hangs in the balance. Once tigers roamed from Turkey eastward through India on to China and Russia. People once revered the magical powers of the cat. The soul of the tiger in life and spirit was part of many cultures. That has changed. Tigers have been exterminated or greatly reduced in number where once they were abundant. Perhaps no more than 5,000 to 6,000 survive in the wild, half of them in India.

India has twenty-eight tiger reserves, but many tigers occur outside such areas as well. Although hunting of the cats has been prohibited since 1970, a time when Prime Minister Indira Gandhi showed great concern for wildlife, protection in recent years has been lax. Tigers continue to be shot, trapped, and poisoned inside and outside of reserves. China and some other Asian countries import tiger bones for use in medicines. A few years ago, some Tibetan people suddenly wanted tiger and leopard skins to decorate their cloaks. Skins came mostly from India. This has had a devastating effect. Tiger numbers in various reserves crashed to a pitiful low or vanished entirely. Prime Minister Manmohan Singh is now supervising a conservation effort to halt the decline of an animal that symbolizes India's natural heritage.

Governments alone cannot save the tiger. Every community, every individual, must somehow contribute to assure the tiger a future. Belinda Wright has shown how one person can make a difference: she started an organization, the Wildlife Protection Society of India, to help tigers. The Hindu goddess Durga rides a tiger to defeat the evil that afflicts the world. The destruction of the environment, its forests and wildlife, is a great evil. Using religion, pride, moral conviction, passion, and everlasting commitment, we must show our loyalty to the tiger and all living beings that share the earth with us and assure their survival.

Agasthyamalai's Sacred Slope

Ian Lockwood

The boy next to me, a young pilgrim with a fragile frame, is muttering a prayer. It is barely discernable over the sounds of thunder and rain lashing down on us. A ferocious wind is sweeping in from the north-east and threatens to blow us off the precipitous summit that we are camping on. Lightning illuminates gnarled trees and the profiles of my companions huddled under a tarp. It leaks like a sieve, but we're holding on to it with all hands, lest the wind blows away our only sense of security. The pilgrim prays on. He is addressing Lord Agasthya, the great sage whose mountain we are on, and probably asking for a quick change of weather.

Agasthyamalai, at 1,866 metres, is the highest point in the southernmost tip of India and one of the richest biodiversity zones in the entire Western Ghats. A stone's throw to the west, the mountain drops for a perilous 700 metres: straight down into the tropical forests of Kerala. The drop on the other three sides is little better, and none of us are happy about the idea of a sudden evacuation. Normally, visitors don't stay overnight on this magnificent peak and, if the weather is anything to go by, the gods aren't pleased with our choice of a camping spot.

I first saw Agasthyamalai's distinctive profile in the carefree years before I had to find a career, earn a living, and be a respectable adult. I was exploring the Kalakkad Mundanthurai Tiger Reserve, seeking to photograph the little-known landscapes of the Western Ghats. My budget was limited; I lived out of a backpack and travelled by state transport buses. On a journey between Courtallam and Mundanthurai I was mesmerized by my first encounter with Agasthyamalai. Swirling monsoon clouds parted to reveal a pointed granite peak high above the hills of the Mundanthurai plateau.

It reminded me of the Palni Hills range to the north, where I had grown up. My friends and I had been a motley bunch of school misfits, who disliked classroom learning and spent as much time in the hill forests as we could. We'd hike to a favourite peak or valley—such as Gundar Valley or Vembadi Peak—and look for places that were free of the ubiquitous eucalyptus plantations and logging operations that had so radically changed the landscape of the Palnis. These areas of the hills offered the best chances of observing the enigmatic wildlife of the Western Ghats. The experiences stayed with me and shaped my adult efforts to record the threatened landscapes of this marvellous part of India.

It is now several years later and I am still in search of adventure and a reunion with Agasthya's distinguished peak. I have managed to obtain the required permission from two state governments as well as the central authorities in New Delhi. My team is made up of five friends from the Dhonavur Fellowship, a community with strong conservation ties in these hills. Jerry Rajamanian, their leader, has a special interest in Pothigai (the Tamil name of Agasthyamalai) and has been instrumental in organizing this expedition. We are supported by several men of the Kani tribe, who will guide us to the summit and help carry food.

Our four-day expedition to Agasthyamalai starts at the Karaiyar reservoir in Kalakkad. Built in the 1960s as part of a massive hydroelectric scheme, the reservoir is surrounded by steep hills carpeted in dense evergreen forest. Protruding from these hills is a jagged ridge of granite peaks that includes the pyramid-shaped Agasthyamalai. An Indian darter flies overhead, yet another reminder that we have left cities and crowds far behind. Jerry, happy as a clam in mud, is documenting the scene with his video camera. His brother Ezekiel seems to be nervously contemplating the height that we will be ascending. Their thin and tall dentist friend Dr Abraham is confident about the walk, but endures the boat ride nervously (he doesn't swim). Two brothers from near Nagercoil, Edison and Dilip Daniel, are also with us. Edison is an English teacher at the Dhonavur

School and Dilip, a biologist, is studying mosses in the southern haunts of the Western Ghats.

Our boat approaches the sandy shore littered with leaf debris and huge blackened tree stumps. A wide waterfall cascades over house-sized boulders before emptying into the dark waters of the reservoir. This is the sacred Tambraparani river. Its watershed is made up of the forested slopes of Agasthyamalai. We clamber up ancient rock-cut steps on the side of the falls. Steep and slippery, they discourage casual explorations beyond the falls. Two fairy bluebirds and a group of ruby-throated black-crested bulbuls flutter in a low tree by the stream. We can just about see the summit of Agasthyamalai peering over the canopy of trees; an awesome sight. Our excitement level soars.

Manikandi, the most knowledgeable of the Kani men, leads us along the river and then cuts up into the forest on a small path. From the scorching heat of the open, we enter the shaded, cool world of the rainforest. Gigantic canes and towering lianas crowd between large buttressed trees. Cicadas fill the air with their deafening calls. Our destination is the Kani tribal settlement of Injukuli. Kanis, the indigenous forest dwellers of the Agasthyamalai hills, once practised shifting cultivation, but many have been relocated out of the protected areas in the interiors of the tiger reserve. In the 1990s they were the focus of much media attention when they struck a deal with a pharmaceutical company to cultivate the Arogyapacha (*Trichopus zeylanicus*) plant. This medicinal plant grows wild on the Kerala side of the Agasthyamalai hills and is said to be a great energizer.

Injukuli consists of a dozen scattered thatched huts and cleared fields, just below the imposing Agasthyamalai. We set up camp near a house owned by a friendly Kani family. Their three children lead us down to the Tambraparani and show us the best spots for an afternoon dip. We turn in early, knowing that tomorrow's trek will make a huge demand on our muscles and will power. Above us, suspended in a cloudless sky, is the waning moon.

The early sunrise casts a crimson glow over the towering trees and cliffs that enclose the settlement. At seven-thirty we strike out on a disused path that winds its way from Injukuli up the Tambraparani and over several valleys to the base of the massive Agasthyamalai. The first bit of the trail takes us through a dense evergreen forest with an exquisite understory and towering trees. The *Cullenia excelsa* tree, much favoured by lion-tailed macaques, is abundant. Most pleasing to me are the dry conditions and absence of leeches. A white-bellied treepie is calling noisily in the canopy just above us. Several hours later we reach Pongalam, a stream-fed pool that offers the last source of water on the way up to the summit. Dense *Ochlandra* reed brakes (a favourite haunt of elephants) surround the pool. We rehydrate on a homemade concoction of electrolytes, feast on tamarind rice, and rest before taking on Agasthyamalai.

After Pongalam, the path ascends at a dizzying angle up the exposed sheet rock that forms the almost vertical eastern face of Agasthyamalai. At times we are forced to proceed on all fours. Clearly this would be quite tricky during the rainy season. The path passes through clumps of the stunted tropical evergreen forest that are distinctive to the slopes of Agasthyamalai and its neighbouring peaks. Severe wind keeps the canopy low and ancient trees are deceptively short and stunted. We see the endemic *Bentickia condapanna* palm trees clinging to precarious slopes. They appear strangely out of place here, as if Dr Seuss had painted them on to the mountainside! A group of brown-backed needletails and other lesser swifts are darting in huge circles over our heads. I look in vain in the grassy clumps for the enigmatic ladyslipper orchid which is restricted to the slopes of Agasthyamalai and is, perhaps, the rarest epiphyte in the entire Western Ghats chain. Just as I'm dreaming about stumbling across one, I spot several large clumps of a bright pink orchid and am content taking pictures of them.

After walking under an enormous wall of charcoal-black sheet rock, we find ourselves approaching the main north-south ridge of the mountain. Now in thick dwarf forest, we join the more worn and used trail from Pepara on the Kerala side of the mountain. It is late afternoon and I am perspiring heavily. I get ahead of the group and emerge on the exposed shoulder of Agasthyamalai. The view around me is spectacular. I can see right across from the Mundanthurai valley clear around the mountain to the western side. To the south the lesser peaks protrude from the forest in a dazzling array of weathered granite and windswept vegetation. Contrary to our expectations, there's practically no wind. There are big thunderstorms in the distance, but the peak is enjoying what seems like a rare calm.

The final approach to the summit is straightforward,

although there are a few unnerving rock faces to get up. I pass a group of pilgrims at a particularly difficult spot. A few more steep bits and then a final patch of forest. And now here I am, standing on top of Agasthyamalai, absolutely elated by the panorama spread before me. The summit is dome-shaped, with a pile of rocks at the high point. Visitors have vandalized it by painting their names on the rock in an ugly shade of yellow. On the southern side of the summit a small crown of forest protects the modest Agasthya deity. He is a short, stout god with a healthy stomach and long beard, protected only by a circular metal shade.

By the time we set up camp it is twilight, and the best camping spot, protected by a ring of trees, has been taken. We find a sloped patch of grass nearby and are able to tie down our large tarp. Meanwhile, two or three different thunderstorms are lashing the eastern plains and the ranges south of Agasthyamalai. It's definitely going to pour. Knowing that we are on the highest peak in the area, I can't help being nervous about what is in store for us.

We enjoy a subdued sunset and a murky moonrise behind layers of thick clouds. When it emerges later, the moon casts an ethereal glow over the hills and approaching thunderheads. The storm moves closer and we take refuge under the tarp, eat a dinner of biscuits, and prepare for the inevitable. It hits around eight-thirty, starting with ferocious winds that threaten to blow our cover off the mountain. At the first gust the ten of us under the tarp grab its corners and folds. For the next two hours we cling to our scanty cover. Lightning bolts strike all around us and light up silhouettes of the wind-blown trees. Thunder rolls through the valleys around Agasthyamalai. We discover another small problem: the tarp leaks horribly! Sitting up in my sleeping bag I put on my rain jacket and contemplate taking out my umbrella. However, there is no room for this luxury and I'm soon drenched. The second group of pilgrims, all six of them, decides to take cover with us and it's a cozy gathering, to say the least! They are surprised and dismayed by nature's fury, and suggest that Agasthya is irritated by our invasion of the summit.

The storm does eventually clear and by midnight we are left with the sounds of water dripping through the tarp and bush frogs croaking in the grass. My sleep is erratic at best. I wake every hour or so, excited by the prospects of dawn and a new day. I know that the rain will have washed the plains and mountains. I'm eager to see and photograph it all!

I get up and out of the slushy sleeping bag at 4.30 a.m. A poncho has protected my cameras, and I move them out to the summit area. A light breeze is blowing and there is still a magical other-worldly glow from the setting moon. The lights from towns on the eastern plains twinkle brilliantly and the brighter constellations are visible. I want to see the view in the complete darkness and witness dawn from the very first light. Jerry, also a view-freak, joins me. We locate both Tirunelveli in the east and Trivandrum in the west, identified by their large clusters of pulsating lights. Four different lighthouses are visible, demarcating the Arabian Sea in the west and the Gulf of Mannar in the east.

Dawn is a magnificent affair on Agasthyamalai's summit and compensates the fear and discomfort of the stormy night. The first rays of the new day paint the cirrus clouds in fantastic hues of gold and scarlet. A kestrel hovers over the precipice near the summit, grey-breasted laughing thrushes chatter in the trees by the Agasthya shrine. Thanks to the night's showers, the plains and hills are astoundingly clear. Looking north, we are blessed with a terrific view of the dark evergreen forests of the Mundanthurai range. The azure mountain ranges stretching beyond the Shencottah Gap and up towards Periyar Tiger Reserve are striking.

Then something incredible happens. The sun, just a hair above the horizon, projects the conical shadow of Agasthyamalai into the light haze of the west. It creates a surreal pyramid-shaped shadow that shifts as I walk along the summit. This is a phenomenon often observed by mountaineers on high peaks at sunrise. I've witnessed it on Adam's Peak in Sri Lanka, but this is the first time I've seen it happening in the Western Ghats in such an extraordinary fashion. The magical shadow doesn't last longer than ten minutes and disappears when the sun slips behind a low cloud.

The pilgrims head down almost immediately, while we linger to dry things out and enjoy the view. Jerry and I work on identifying the local peaks. As the sun rises higher, we are thrilled to spot both coastlines! The dark blues of the seas are distinctly visible.

By mid-morning a wispy mist is gathering at Agasthyamalai's summit and we make a move down the mountainside. The night's rain has made the rock faces slippery, and we proceed with great caution. I flush a peregrine falcon from a patch of grass. It goes soaring out over the edge and gives its mournful alarm call. Although our knees start to feel like jelly, the descent takes much less effort than yesterday's climb. At Pongalam I use the opportunity to bathe in the pool and am soon convinced about the divine properties of the ritual! We are back in Injukuli by late afternoon. Our final day in the shadow of Agasthyamalai goes smoothly. We pack up and say thank you to the Kanis. It is a gentle path back to Banerthetum and I walk most of it alone.

Since that time, I have been in jungles and mountains many, many more times. I've seen and photographed exotic and wonderful animals such as Nilgiri tahr, rare pit vipers, gliding frogs and more. But that journey to Agasthyamalai holds a very special place in my memory. It was, in a sense, a true pilgrimage and I, the pilgrim, returned with an even stronger belief in the magic and power of nature, and the need to protect it.

Zoo Girl

Sally Walker

When I left California in the early 1970s, my destination was Mysore, India and my objective to study yoga, pranayama and Sanskrit until I felt confident enough to teach. Then I was going to hotfoot it back to California and set up a yoga studio for the Hollywood stars, or something. I never imagined doing anything else.

So it was with some surprise that I found myself in the Mysore Zoo taking care of chimpanzee babies, taming tigers, playing with otters, and conducting teacher training courses. How did I get there—from yoga to zoos? It's a tame enough story actually.

I studied yoga in Patabhi Jois's yogashala for six years. Yes six years, daily, twice a day with pranayama. After about four years, I added a different style of yoga, that of B.K.S. Iyengar. It was back-breakingly and mind-bendingly exhausting and painful. I loved it. But the day came after six years when all my yoga teachers (I had three by that time) abandoned me. Why? They went to U.S.A. to teach. Naturally they would.

I did not feel I was ready to teach yoga even after six years and was moping about wondering what to do, when I saw a notice in the Mysore afternoon rag, the *Star of Mysore*, stating that three baby tiger cubs in the zoo were 'ready for handling'. Ha! ready for handling? Well, I wanted to handle a tiger cub. I loved animals. I loved animals so much that I had never visited the zoo. I didn't like to see animals in cages. I decided to make an exception for this rare privilege of 'handling' a tiger cub. As if fate wanted to help me, I was invited to a birthday party of a friend that night and he introduced me to his daughter Vasanthi, who was the veterinary officer at the Mysore Zoo. I told her about the notice in the paper and she gulped and said, 'Well, actually it meant handling by our own keepers, not outsiders, but I'll see what I can do . . .'

The next day I went to the zoo and stopped at Vasanthi's office at the appointed time. She had suggested I come when the tiger cage needed cleaning as that was the time the keeper took the cubs out for a while. She took me to the tiger cages and introduced me to the tiger keeper, Kempalinga, who brought me a tiger cub about six weeks old. A six-week-old tiger cub is just the right age to kill you with terminal cuteness. I was intrigued and impressed. A cat lover all my life, this was kind of an 'ultimate cat'. I went back the next day about the same time, walked up to the cage and looked longingly through the bars. Kempalinga was there and, thinking I was very influential since I knew the zoo vet, brought the cub out and put her in my arms. I kept her while he cleaned the cage, and felt so very useful. I sat under a tree and gazed at her like a lovesick teenager. I saw God and I was in love—I had fallen in love with a tiger cub. I went back day after day and kept Rukmani for half an hour. Soon other cubs grew big enough to take out and I was babysitting four of them in an outdoor pen, so that visitors could see them up close. I think visitors were more interested in me, a crazy foreigner in a cage with tiger cubs, but I didn't care because by now I was fascinated with the growth and behaviour of these wonderful animals.

More tiger cubs appeared and soon there were seven! I noticed by then that the keepers believed you had to frighten the cubs and knock them around a bit to show them who was boss. I didn't think this was right. I was sure that being kind but firm would go further. And it did. I got permission to experiment, to stay in the cage with the seven cubs several hours a day, observe their behaviour, play with them and be kind but firm. My goal was to demonstrate to the keepers that you could get more control over the cubs with this method than with fear. It worked.

After six or eight months, these cubs were BIG! They were big enough to be dangerous if they had a mind to. I played with them as if they were pups or kittens, with certain differences.

I was careful not to run away from them; I could play only by chasing, not being chased. I tried never to turn my back to them—that would only tempt them. I also stayed out of the way of their teeth and claws during play.

These cubs were very friendly to me, but that courtesy didn't extend to the keepers. When I entered the cage, they would all come up to me making the charming little snorting or puffing sound that is called 'prustin', and is a sort of 'hello friend' of several felines. Sometimes I took a keeper in with me, including one who thought he had to be tough to be safe. The behaviour of the cubs was entirely different towards him. They would gather in a group and start growling and snarling at him. He couldn't approach them, but I could go to them and sit down in the middle of their snarling group. They recognized and trusted me. It was a wonderful feeling to be trusted and befriended by such powerful animals.

Although these big cubs clearly didn't want to hurt me, they were indeed very powerful, so I had to protect THEM from hurting ME by being careful. When they were a year old, I stopped going inside the cage with them. I wasn't frightened of them but frightened for them. Wild animals will definitely bond with and love human beings, but you can never predict their lightning fast reaction if some stimulus in the environment seems threatening to them. Their wild life has given them these skills for protection.

Most of 'my' tiger cubs went to other zoos on animal exchange programmes, but Rukmani remained in Mysore Zoo for some years. She was always very tame and a keeper called Mahadeva used to take her from a fairly small cage to an outdoor area with more space, grass and trees by leading her on a rope. Once I was walking through the zoo with a journalist, being interviewed about some conservation issue. We ran right into Mahadeva and Rukmani. Rukmani broke away from Mahadeva and bounded over to me . . . People watching thought I was done for! But Rukmani remembered me and she only wanted a hug. She reared up on her hind legs, put her front paws around my shoulders and gently took the back of my neck in her jaws. Nothing happened, but I thought later how easy it would have been for someone to shout or run towards us and frighten Rukmani just at that moment. She could have taken my head off without even trying . . . without meaning to. It struck me that it was very unfair of human beings to tame animals for their own pleasure. The animals become fond of us but eventually we have to reject them for our mutual safety. If Rukmani had become frightened in the zoo that day and killed me, she might have been shot or injured as keepers rushed to my rescue.

This kind of drama has been played out all too often. People adopt a wild animal and enjoy it while it is young. When it gets big, it is too much animal for a household, and the family gives it to a zoo, or a pet shop, or—worst of all—releases it in the forest where it doesn't know how to survive. Now there are strict laws against catching or buying wild animals and keeping them as pets.

In the last couple of years, there have been several instances of big cats attacking their human friends. One such incident was at the Siegfried and Roy Circus in the United States. Neither the victim of the attack, nor his brother blamed the tiger, simply saying it was a 'stochastic' event, a random and unfortunate combination of disturbances not perceived by human senses. Feeling threatened, the tiger acted instinctively, which didn't make it a 'bad' animal. Every time I hear one of these stories, I feel very grateful that this never happened to me. I am grateful to be alive and unmaimed and also grateful that I never got a tiger in trouble. After all, tigers are the ultimate cats!

Meroe: The Rumbling Island

Manish Chandi

It was a hot February afternoon in 2001 and I was on Pulomilo, one of the small southern islands in the Nicobar archipelago. With me were Robinson, the keeper of the lighthouse beacon on the island, and his two friends Moses and Albert. We were waiting for a boat to Meroe, where I would continue my sea turtle nest study and this group of Payuh—local southern Nicobarese—would join some others to process copra for sale. Meroe belongs to the people of Little Nicobar and is one of their plantation islands. But it's more than just another one of their coconut and areca nut farms . . .

It's magical; Meroe is a special island, with unique and wonderful natural features. In its centre is a salty lake. The lake isn't fed by a visible inlet, like normal estuarine lakes, but by an underground channel! Another wonder is that the island shakes and rumbles from time to time; when this happens, water in the lake rises and falls. Crocodiles and dolphins—and once, a reticulated python—have been seen in and around it. Near the banks, large lianas twine around the trees, and legend has it that the vegetation here is so thick and tangled that people lose their way and go round in circles forever, like the lianas. There was much to see on Meroe and I couldn't wait to get there. The island has only one landing beach, and Robinson had offered to drop us there along with our rations and pick us up (and the processed copra) after a week.

Early the next morning we carried our rations into the dingy, a low-slung canoe-like boat used for inter-island travel in the Andaman and Nicobar archipelago. I squeezed in between bags, bundles and bodies. We punted over the shallow reef until we hit deeper water, and then the engine putted to life and put us on the sea-swell, as the sun began a slow rise over the purple-orange sky. The sky colours changed every few minutes, and a light sea spray hit us with each wave. Moses and Co. were letting out trawl lines with lures of chicken feathers. Soon there was a shout; the first of many mackerel had been hooked and our lunch was secured.

Shoals of them dived in front of the boat, chasing minnows, and we soon had two more. Then the lines had to be pulled in as the sea surface changed; we were passing through a rip tide. This is a mid-sea drama, a clash of strong currents from many directions. Robinson tugged at the tiller as the dinghy was buffeted, then pulled along the tide stream. As we slowed down, Albert spoke of a custom in force before motorized boats travelled these seas. When the Nicobarese sailed in canoes to islands like Meroe, legends reminded them to keep still and not fight or shout on board, but to work as a team. There were creatures of the deep that would, if irritated, bounce out of the water and swallow you up or overturn your boat. There were giant octopi that could yank the boat into the deep, big box-like fish that would knock about and play with the boat like a toy, and enormous eel-like creatures that could pull the canoe out to sea and set the men on a lost course. It all seemed so real and possible, with the rip streams tossing our little dinghy between small unwieldy swells. Soon we were out of the tide stream and the boat chugged on past two small islets—Mataanh and Mafuii[1], sister islands, each with white sandstone cliffs staring at us like startled eyes. In between was a large rock protruding out of the water like an unfortunately large nose.

With the morning haze giving way to clear sunshine, Meroe island became visible. In the far distance were two sticks and white flapping cloth. They were the sails of the canoes that had left Pulomilo much before us, also heading for Meroe. The sails were gathering wind and ballooning nicely.

---

[1]These two islets are mapped as Treis and Trak islets. The names originate from Portuguese or Danish sailors who explored these regions two centuries ago.

I was sure that our motorized engine would soon catch up with these ancient contraptions, but was mistaken. With the wind strengthening as the morning came on, the sails pulled the light canoes faster than our slick engine.

In another hour we were close to Meroe. I could see flat rocky outcrops along the western shore and a tall cliff stepping into the sea, darkened by its own shadow and lashed by waves below. All of a sudden, there was a foamy splash ahead of the dinghy. A sinewy body leaped into the air, smirking at the sun. Dolphins—by the dozen—were escorting us, cutting the surface with their fins and diving in to come up on the other side. The entire school moved as one mass, synchronizing their movements with those of an unseen leader . . . who suddenly decided enough was enough. The entire school vanished into the deep. The canoes were ahead, sails lowered and waiting for us. They would transport us to the beach, as the dinghy was too heavy to navigate the shallows.

Robinson steered the dinghy close along Meroe's cliff shore, so I could see its dramatic landforms. He pointed out the cavernous entrances along the coast where waves swelled and broke in a deep rumbling clap, spraying water and salt every half minute. Coconut trees filled the bottom of the cliff and thinned out closer to the beach. Other large trees appeared here and there, while tufts of tall bamboo clumps stuck out like brushes in the green canopy. A pair of sea eagles took off from their tree perch and circled above us as we prepared to land. I thought our landing place would be a beautiful curved beach, but realized it was to be a bay fringed by sharp rocks sticking out like thorns in the water. There were more craggy shoals and rock outcrops before we reached the canoes, with a triumphant shout from Robinson.

We drew alongside the sleek canoes well balanced by their outriggers. Calvin, Fred, Bernard and Saul welcomed us with the broad, vigorous smiles of the Nicobarese. The transfer of people and luggage in wobbly boats isn't easy, but the Payuh have been doing it for hundreds, maybe thousands of years. The dinghy was tied to one of the canoes, and I straddled its gunwale and jumped into the canoe behind Albert. I was to row quick and fast, then jump off in the shallows to help pull the canoe up the beach. We were the first to go and with a shove from Robinson's foot, we dug our oars into the water. A strong wave from behind pushed us forward, another lifted us up. A few more strokes, and we had the canoe on the beach. The other canoe followed, after Robinson had anchored his dinghy beyond the breakers.

There were two huts on stilts, one falling apart but the other intact. We stashed our luggage and began to clean up and cook. Our beach was a small indentation along the otherwise rocky coast, and the soft white sand was heating up. A constant breeze surged in from the sea. A sharp, rocky moonscape of coralline rock extended from the shore to the sea. Some of the hollows were dry, others filled by the constant splash of waves and rollers breaking along the edge. My mind began searching for metaphors and comparisons. Enormous prehistoric footprints, I decided, placed at random on a coral walkway.

At the base of the cliff was a large hollow, a cave that sucked the sea into darkness with every wave. The climb to the cliff began along this edge of the coast. From where I stood, it looked like a different world.

The hut was at the beginning of a very thick grove of coconuts. Coconut tree trunks were all that was visible, shaded by the unfolding canopy of coconut leaves. I walked into its darkness. The floor was littered with leaves, nuts and old decaying wood that had lain around for months and years. A coconut forest. After a few paces, there was no path and the trees grew so close that in places they were like a wall, leaning on each other. I looked back; it was as dark as my way ahead: I felt lost and without bearings. My mind played tricks. Then I saw a rat, its quivering nose and beady eyes peeping at me from behind a stack of nuts. When I stopped and stared, it flung itself forward and disappeared. I looked around . . . forest lizards peered from behind tree trunks, still as statues but alert. Others hid under cover of the leaves and coconuts sprouting among the ground debris. They were all around. Hermit crabs scurried about crisscrossing each other's paths, with the small ones taking off as bigger ones ambled in their direction. Small mattresses of moss, grass and leaves gave way to a nursery of sprouting coconuts where the trees ended.

Listening to the roar of the sea behind, I made my way back. Salt spray from the sea wind coated virtually every leaf close to shore. Our meal was ready: barbecued fish, coconuts and rice. Biting into a tasty mackerel, I asked Robinson about stories I'd heard about the past inhabitants of Meroe. He nodded silently; this was obviously not to be spoken about on the island. He'd talk about it on the way back to Pulomilo, he said.

We said goodbye to Robinson and his team and waved them off. Five of us remained. Terns hovered above the dinghy and followed in its wake; some looked different and had a call I could not recognize. What were they? We returned to the hut. I was surprised to see a family of domestic chickens: a hen, a rooster and a single chick. Albert explained that a mini poultry farm had been left here for food, but Burmese poachers had polished them off! I walked with him and the others to where they'd be processing copra and then moved on to explore the rest of the island, keeping close to the coast.

I wandered through the brush and the thick trees. The ubiquitous lizards were everywhere, watching me as I passed through the maze of coconut trees and huge fallen tree trunks. Some were in states of decay with moss and lichen growing in profusion and providing a cool, moist, shady niche for many lucky creatures. Hermit crabs abounded; unperturbed by my presence a large purplish male waved its round claw towards me and unfurled its feelers. A fallen coconut was torn, exposing the kernel. Could be the work of rats, I thought, as two guilty rodents ran under the log I was sitting on. Further on, I reached the forest on the cliff slope. It was even darker than the coconut forest, with tall saplings that broke into leaf above my head, reaching for the sun's rays. The trees had gnarled bark and large roots, and the saplings wore invisible spider webs which netted me as I moved through. Now I was on a ridge from where I could see the lake, edged with mangroves. I decided to explore it later, and returned to camp for a nap before a nocturnal beach walk to look for nesting sea turtles.

I woke up as dusk settled in. Calvin had returned from copra-processing and was preparing dinner. The hen and chick were busily picking at scraps, clucking in happiness at the arrival of food and people. At another fire, I made tea for all of us and went down to the beach. The sea had calmed and looked placid, settling down for the night. Over its quiet swells terns and other sea-faring birds navigated the air currents. And here again was the strange new bird. I returned to the hut and looked it up in my bird book. It turned out to be the white-tailed tropicbird, *Phaethon lepturus*. It's such a beautiful feeling, identifying a species you haven't seen before. I spoke of it to the others at tea, and learnt that they'd seen it only around Meroe. They called it Kau kilain.

With darkness came the mosquitoes. At first they made their presence known with a few stings, then clouds of them descended on us and didn't seem to mind the fire or smoke at all. We had to live with them. We sat by the orange glow of the fire, chatting and swatting. Then I saw, by the light of the fire, a few small red glows appear and disappear in the darkness a little distance away. Switching on my torch, I saw rats; tens of them, scurrying about, jumping from branches to fallen nuts, sniffing about for morsels, bumping into others and quarrelling over their space. As I swung the beam around, I found some on bushes, and others climbing up young saplings and hopping towards the beach. Unlike city rats, these were not ugly and intimidating. They were not shy and would sit close to us, nibbling at scraps and twitching their noses. They looked strangely like one another, all the same size, all grey on top with clean white fur on the belly. They seemed to have come alive with the darkness. I wondered about their colonization of the island: how did they get here? Maybe, like the house geckoes I'd seen in the hut, they too had arrived by canoe. Perhaps they were descendents of survivors of a nearby shipwreck. I got sucked into a vortex of speculation. In any case, they'd done well for themselves in this rat-paradise, with plenty of food.

The night wore on and I made sure I had an extra torch with me as I left to scour the small beaches for sea turtles. But I didn't need it; the moon was bright and lit the island like a floodlight. Ghost crabs rummaged for beach fleas and other insects in broken seaweed and decaying flotsam. They ran off at my approach, some into their holes and others into the froth and foam of waves. The flotsam included plastic floats, rubber slippers, rope, toys and bottles from various corners of the earth, drifting to destinations as remote as this beach. Scanning the beach for sea turtle tracks, I found none. I settled down on a rock on the beach to wait. There were only two other coves that sea turtles could visit to lay their eggs. The rest of the coast was rock and reef. I sat and looked out on to the dark sea and listened to the sound of waves breaking.

An hour later I saw a movement. It was a snake emerging from the sea. It slid sideways on the soft sandy beach, climbed up to the edge of the vegetation, and curled up under a young screw pine. My torch beam picked up more of them, coiled within buttresses of trees and between small rocks and stones on the floor of this beach forest. They were banded sea kraits (*Laticauda colubrine*), which live on small fish, eel and other prey in the reef. These sea snakes climb ashore to rest after a long swim and to digest food. The females also lay their eggs on shore, under forest debris. *Laticauda* are deadly poisonous, but bite only under extreme provocation. It's easy to identify the males, as they are much smaller and thinner than the females.

I moved on, walking for many hours along the three coves with beaches. No turtles. I contemplated returning to camp, but told myself to be patient and hang on. There were rats and ghost crabs for company, rummaging about the debris of the beach and forest floor, the rats squeaking in excitement over disputed territory. Beach hoppers hid between flotsam; some burrowed themselves into the wet sand as a wave washed the shore. Hermit crabs, those tireless scavengers, slogged up and down the moonlit beach, moving from the shore into thickets and then back. Their tracks resemble those of sea turtles, but in miniature form. A large number of them had converged to feast on a pandanus fruit, their shells knocking together as they shoved and pushed for space. I left them at their gastronomic orgy and dozed.

It was well past midnight when I awoke. I took another walk along the three small beaches, but saw no signs of sea turtles. On one of the beaches I saw what looked like the track of a cat or a civet; outlines of paws were clearly visible, and they were fresh. Tired and shivering in the early morning wind, I decided to get back to camp and return the next night.

Waking up after sunrise, I saw a few mosquitoes on my net. On closer inspection, I found that they were not on the net but inside, in large numbers. I deftly slipped out and gleefully gathered the netting for a massacre of mosquitoes. Fred, one of the Payuh, had returned from the beach with two fish-jacks or trevallies he'd caught by casting a line just off the reef. I asked him about the pugmarks I'd seen, and was told about two cats introduced on the island to take care of the rats. They had obviously failed miserably in their task!

Sitting in the hut, I planned my routine: explore different sections of the island for birds and other animal life during the day, and spend portions of the night walking the small beaches to record sea turtle arrivals. This would give me enough time to rest and to fraternize with my new friends.

For the next few days, I explored the cliff, the lake and the forest, crisscrossing the island between coast and jungle. The others were busy smoke-drying mature coconuts into copra. They also brought large numbers for us to snack on. The coconuts attracted rats, ants, hermit crabs and the largest crab on earth: the robber crab (*Birgus latro*). Albert trapped one to show me. He lifted an overturned metal bucket weighed down with a large rock and a 'robber' emerged and spread out its claws menacingly. Its grip on the metal handle of the bucket was strong and vice-like. It stood its ground, not ready to give any quarter. I photographed it as Albert deftly held it up for a comparison of size, then let it go. They'd found it under a log which they picked up to use as firewood to process copra. These crabs forage for food on the forest floor, including fallen coconuts. They are gigantic cousins of hermit crabs; only, they can never find a shell large enough to fit their bodies!

During one of my walks in the coastal forest, I came across a bird unique to the Nicobar islands, the Nicobar megapode. They move in pairs, foraging on the forest floor, and construct large mounds of sand, mud and debris to incubate their eggs. I saw three megapodes; one pair and a single bird. According to traditional law, the Payuh may not hunt these birds and other species such as the robber crab on outlying islands. Disobedience, they believe, will bring either physical harm or illness of the mind and spirit.

These long-established eco-friendly laws had been practised by the Nicobarese for generations. This was why the forests and wildlife of the Nicobar islands had remained healthy. Animals and plants were sacred, and must be selectively and wisely used. It was animism at its best. When Christianity and other religions reached the shores of the Nicobars, many islanders adopted them, wanting to switch over to modern, progressive lifestyles. Healthy traditional foods like pandanus gave way to rice, sugar, and tea. I met some elders who refuse to eat non-traditional food, and live on fish, boar, coconuts, pandanus and toddy. But things are changing. Soon Nicobarese culture will be a thing of the past, and the placid life by the sea will be replaced by the stress of modern commerce and industry. I was lucky to be there in the twilight years of Nicobarese culture.

On the fourth night of my stay on Meroe, I came across sea turtles nesting. The moon was waning, the night dark and windy. The sea crashed noisily against the rocks on either side of the little beach I was sitting on. Then, I saw a turtle appear through the surf . . . suddenly, as though it hadn't swum but just popped up from the depths of the sea. It looked shiny black, darkened by the dim light and the wash of the waves. It lunged ashore, swinging its fore flippers in front and pulling itself up the beach with each heave. I did not approach it, but waited for it to settle down. It was a green sea turtle. As I watched, another smaller turtle climbed further up the beach. I walked over; it was a hawksbill, also known to nest on this island. These two sea turtle species nest on both small and large beaches, whereas the leatherback and the olive ridley prefer larger and wider beaches. The last two also nest in the Andaman and Nicobar islands, though their nesting beaches are few because of the rapid and skewed 'development' of this beautiful eco-system. The Andaman-Nicobar archipelago remains the only nesting area of the leatherback in India.

Two more green sea turtles arrived in the wee hours of the morning, and over the next few days I saw many more. One afternoon after a visit to the lake, I walked slowly through the forest and found my way with some difficulty to the slope of the cliff. It wasn't steep, but thickets of thorny screw pine made it tough going. The view from the top was exhilarating. I could see Little Nicobar in the distance, and a cargo ship sailing south in international waters. The sea was as blue as can be; a few white caps marked wave crests breaking in the wind. The white-tailed tropicbirds flew about close by, and on spotting me, began calling and moved closer, swooping in to have a better look. I lay down and placed my chin on the edge of the cliff. It was steep as a wall and below me I could see the clear blue water and even count large fish swimming. A few tropicbirds landed on the cliff face below me and disappeared inside. Very little is known about this bird. Its distribution on the Indian subcontinent is recorded as 'from the Nicobar islands' without specifying an exact locality in the archipelago. Meroe, which has a breeding population, is the only island known to harbour this species. Other small outlying islands in the Nicobars, such as Battimalv and the Isle of Man, may have small populations as well.

I began my return before sunset, gaily traipsing along the edge of the cliff. There were pigeons landing on trees close by: pied imperial pigeons. Draped in white and black finery, they made a pretty sight among the green trees and blue sky. On moving further, I saw a pair on a branch just above my head, in what looked like a nest. On seeing me they took off. These birds can nest close to the ground on Meroe as there are no predators, unlike on the larger islands where macaques, snakes and monitor lizards may gobble up the eggs. On another evening I saw the pigeons arriving on Meroe in flocks of up to twenty, to roost for the night. They left early in the morning to feed on fruit on Little Nicobar island, and returned again before dark.

The wind was now much stronger during the day than when we had first landed. Our week was nearly up, and we realized we'd be stuck if the wind continued to buffet the shore. We would not be able to launch the canoes, nor would Robinson be able to land. Our supply of water was nearly finished. And then, on the day Robinson was expected, it began to rain. The wind picked up, throwing sea spray right into the huts. It was funny to taste salt in the rain. I wasn't able to go out at night as it poured incessantly. The rain storm lasted another two days. We had begun to use brackish water from rain pools for cooking, saving the fresh water to drink when we tired of coconuts. The forest of coconuts and native trees changed: the moss turned velvety green, and soggy logs sprouted mushrooms and other fungi. There were less mosquitoes to deal with, but large centipedes came out at night.

Sitting with my Payuh friends under a dripping roof and watching the stormy sea, it was difficult to imagine that I'd soon be back in the land of traffic jams and crowds. It was like being transported to the primordial times of Early Man. This other-worldly feeling was strengthened by occasional mild tremors and rumbles. During one of these rumbles, there was a windy 'whoosh' in the trees; certainly a good place to manufacture ghost stories.

By now, the others had processed a fair amount of copra. They had gone to specific locations and found plantations of different islanders by notches carved on trees, signatures of ownership. They collected nuts from those they owned, and left the others: a rare partnership of trust and honesty. Perhaps it was easier to be honest in this remote archipelago where only necessities could be bought; the rabid consumerism of mainland India hadn't touched these shores. I reflected on my own life and desires.

It was the eleventh day of our stay, and our rations were down to some rice, a bit of salt and tea (but no sugar). Our luck turned at midday, when there was a happy shout of 'BOAT!' We ran out to the beach. Robinson's boat was coming towards us, alongside two canoes with sails billowing in the wind. It was a good sight.

We first loaded the canoes and the dinghy with the copra. Two of us boarded the dinghy along with Robinson and his son, while the rest sailed on the canoes. The two sea eagles of Meroe hovered above, glancing down at us as we sailed away from the island. It was a calm sea that took us back to Pulomilo.

Bob Hoots

Shanthi Chandola

Ashish (my husband), Sitara (our young boxer) and I spend a lot of time on our farm, where we grow aromatic herbs. It's near a little village called Yelashetty, about five kilometres from the Bandipur Tiger Reserve.

If any of you have been to Bandipur you will understand why we chose this spot. Bandipur is a magical place and one can always see scores of chital, monkeys (bonnet macaque and common langur), and enough wild boar to make Asterix and Obelix drool. The monkeys are always entertaining to watch as they, well, monkey around—wrestling on the road, swinging from low branches and even from Mama's tail, making faces and chattering away when nervous. We've seen wild dogs and leopard right on the road to our village. On one occasion we saw a leopard boldly walking into a large herd of chital and picking up a young fawn, while the entire area resounded with the chorus of alarm calls.

Our farm is on the edge of a pond and attracts a lot of birds—kingfishers, dabchicks, grey and purple herons, lesser whistling teal and spot-billed duck, to name a few. There are also a number of smaller birds—the magpie robin, Indian robin, pied bush chat, ashy prinia, tailor bird, red-whiskered and white-browed bulbul, and many more. For a keen birdwatcher, there are always birds to see, nests to find and calls to identify. Our day invariably begins with the 'Three Cheers' from the spotted babbler, and a chorus of competing calls from grey partridge. We wake up early, and walk into the scrub jungle behind our farm. These walks are made compulsory, rain or shine, by Sitara. She trots ahead of us, sniffing and checking out who's been around and drawing our attention to leopard scat and other interesting things.

When we were building our home, our generous friends and neighbours Arun and Anu invited us to use their place. It's a cottage with a tiled roof. And in that tiled roof lived a pair of spotted owlets. When we were away in Bangalore and the house was locked up, the owlets had the run of the place. Every time we came back, we'd find it covered with owl droppings, but the good thing was that they also kept it completely free of rats! The birds would chuckle noisily from time to time, reminding us of their presence. Some time towards the end of March the noisy chuckling and interactions increased, so we suspected that they were now nesting.

Early in April, our own little cottage was ready, so we moved there. In the first week of May, Anu came down for a visit and we went across to see her. She told us that a little spotted owlet chick had fallen into her kitchen and she didn't know what to do with it. Ashish put it back in its nest hole, but the next day the little fellow had fallen down again! This time we couldn't put him back. We were leaving for Bangalore and so was Anu. The house was going to be locked up, and if he fell yet again, he wouldn't be able to get back and would certainly die of starvation.

The chick was almost the size of an adult owl, with fully formed wings, and we guessed that he'd be ready to fledge in a week or two. When we held him, he was most indignant and protested by clicking his beak, screeching and staring at us with baleful yellow eyes. He was a real beauty. We fell in love with him and decided to take him back to Bangalore with us. He was transported in a strong cardboard box with Sitara keeping him company in the back seat of our car.

Our biggest concern was—would he eat? If he did, half the battle would be won. When we got to our home in Whitefield, Bangalore, we boiled an egg and, holding him carefully with his feathers pinned back, offered him some egg white. Surprise, surprise, he was obviously very hungry and eagerly ate the offering. Next we tried some boiled chicken and he seemed to love that too! This was great and we only had to be careful not to overfeed him.

After feeding him and making sure that all the windows were shut, we let him free and he showed off his newly acquired flying skills. He explored the kitchen counter and windowsill, and inspected the light fittings. That night we decided to leave him free in the basement. It had no door, but we didn't expect him to wander too much on his first night in a new place.

At five-thirty the next morning I heard him calling and went down. There was no sign of him in the basement. A thorough search of the ground floor also turned up nothing. It was no easy task as we had to look in every nook and cranny, inspect every piece of furniture. It took us two hours to find him . . . behind the filing cabinet on the first floor!

Sitara was very intrigued with this guy who got chicken or boiled egg at every meal—why didn't she?!—and she kept trying to give him her paw to encourage him to play with her. He in turn bobbed his head and made funny faces at all of us. Birds fluff themselves up to look big and intimidating, bob their heads and stare at the offender. We decided to honour this endearing behaviour, and name him Bob Hoots.

Within a couple of days we had all settled into the new routine. Bob would be fed twice or thrice a day. After his initial adventure of exploring our house, he was confined to a cardboard box after breakfast. Between 5 and 8 p.m. he had the run of the ground floor, and when it was bedtime for us, he'd give us quite a chase before we caught and put him into the guest room for the night. He very quickly settled on the ceiling fan as his favourite perch.

But Bob soon outgrew his cardboard box and made it plain that he didn't like to be confined in there. So, he alternated between the guest bedroom and the guest bathroom.

He enjoyed his meals, and ate his chicken pieces with a look of utter bliss. I would hold him in my hand, and he was very gentle while accepting a piece of chicken or just visiting. We were worried that his diet was a bit monotonous and kept requesting our old gardener (Thatha) to try and catch some grasshoppers, but Thatha with his bad eyesight was not very successful. Our plan was to take Bob Hoots back to Bandipur and release him there, but in the meantime, he needed to learn to hunt and eat on his own.

Meanwhile, something interesting was happening outside our home. Whitefield is still quite rural and has more birds and animals compared to the rest of Bangalore. We see and hear the occasional grey partridge—or grey francolin as they are called these days—and even spot an occasional black naped hare. The colony we live in has only ten houses and many empty plots, and we'd seen quite a few spotted owlets around.

On 27 May 2007, three spotted owlets (possibly Mom, Dad and chick) moved closer to us and took up residence in the teak trees outside our home. There seemed to be quite a lot of communication between Bob and the family outside, and for the first time we heard a low contact call, kind of like a 'krrrrrrrh'. We wondered whether they thought him an intruder or a friend and tried to encourage him to join them by leaving the bedroom windows open every evening.

One evening, Sitara and I were sitting on the front steps,

watching the open bedroom window. One of the adult spotted owlets flew on to a post directly opposite the window. There was a lot of contact calling and Bob responded by positioning himself on the curtains. Then, just as we thought he might fly, Sitara went to the window and put up her paw, sending him back inside. This happened twice that evening; then as it was getting dark, we decided that this wasn't Bob's lucky day. We shut the window for the night. A little later it started to rain.

While I was making chappatis, I noticed that the shut kitchen window was crawling with aelates. Aelates are winged termites, which break out of the earth after a shower. The rain helps to loosen the soil and the aelates come out in thousands. If this happens during daylight, birds like crows, mynahs, brahminy kites, and drongos feast on them. At night nocturnal birds like owls enjoy this highly nutritious and protein-packed dinner. Aelates are attracted to light and that is why they were swarming outside our kitchen window. I called to Ashish, who was working on the computer upstairs. He went out and collected some in a container.

Bob was in the bathroom and we were eager to see whether he would eat the aelates. He took to them like a veteran and devoured thirty in one sitting! We again kept the bedroom and bathroom windows open for the next few days, hoping that he would join the owlets outside. But Bob preferred the safety of his bedpost, fan and loft. We decided he'd know best when and where he wanted to leave us—here in Whitefield or back home in Bandipur. We were returning to Bandipur on 31 May and would take him back with us. As you can imagine, we'd grown very fond of the little fellow—and so had Sitara, who made it a point to check on him from time to time.

By now, we were experiencing pre-monsoon showers and there was no dearth of aelates. On the evening of the 28th, we just left a cupful of them in the bathroom and did not hand-feed Bob like we normally did. We left the bathroom door open a crack and watched like proud parents as he hopped on to the counter and helped himself. When he'd finished the ones on the counter, he hopped to the floor and finished any that had tried to escape. Hurrah! Bob was making great progress.

29th May: We had gone into town and, returning home at about 7.30 p.m., couldn't find Bob in any of his favourite places. Maybe he was on the floor eating aelates? Ashish went to check and called out 'He's gone!'

Then I heard that low contact call 'krrrrrrrh', and there he was—perched on the electric wire outside. We ran upstairs to get a better look from our balcony. We called out to him and he moved closer while Ashish took a photograph.

Then, as we watched, one of the adult spotted owlets flew up and joined Bob on the wire. We watched incredulously as the adult bird fed him at least five times within the next half hour! I was watching through binoculars and Ashish was taking photographs. We could see the blissed-out expression on Bob's face as he feasted on a green grasshopper. We were absolutely delighted—this was far better than anything we could have hoped for. Now there were four spotted owlets on the wire. After watching them for an hour, we decided to go down and have some dinner ourselves.

30 May: At 5.45 a.m. there was quite a commotion outside, with six spotted owlets on the wire! Bob was being chased a bit and came down to the hibiscus hedge. I ran down to get to him in case he was being pecked, but before I could get to the garden he'd flown up again and sat next to one of his adopted parents. That seemed to sort the equation out. Maybe it was the neighbours checking out the new arrival. After the initial excitement they left, and the family of four settled down to spend the day in the foliage of the teak trees.

So, Bob was free and had a new family to take care of him, but was still visible from our bedroom. He'd spent twenty-one days with us and given us so much joy. It had been a wonderful interlude in our lives.

Turning the Tide

Kartik Shanker

Imagine yourself on a beach in Orissa in winter. Moonlight glistens and is reflected, not off the sand or water but off the wet backs of a thousand turtles! Each olive ridley, two feet long and weighing about fifty kilograms, has dragged itself up the beach to dig a nest and lay eggs, as all sea turtles do. Unlike other sea turtles though, ridleys indulge in an annual ritual known as the arribada, which means 'arrival' in Spanish. Tens of thousands come ashore at the same time to lay their eggs. This amazing natural phenomenon may disappear one day unless we are able to do something about the hazards that threaten these turtles' very existence.

Sea turtles are magical animals, all the more mystifying because of our ignorance about them. They appear but briefly on land to fulfil their reproductive duties, and spend the rest of their lives wandering the oceans. As hatchlings, they drift with oceanic currents, sometimes traversing the entire Pacific or Atlantic. When they become adults ten to fifteen years later (some species live up to fifty years), they use the earth's magnetic field to find and lay their eggs on the same beach where they were born!

They have done this for millions of years. But today, sea turtles are threatened by human activity. This includes the increasing pollution of the oceans. Electric lights on beaches confuse and disorient hatchlings and prevent them from finding the ocean after they hatch. Fishing nets have killed hundreds of thousands of turtles worldwide; sea turtles are air breathers and when they get accidentally caught in fishing nets, they drown. In Orissa, more than 100,000 olive ridleys have been killed in trawl fishing nets in the last ten years. Current efforts to create an alliance between fishermen and conservationists seem to offer some hope.

I saw my first olive ridley turtle one moonlit night in Chennai. We had just started a student group to conserve turtles. We watched the female turtle come ashore, crawl up to a dry part of the beach, dig a two-feet deep nest with her hind flippers, and lay 100 to 150 eggs. The hatchlings would emerge about two months later, and under the cover of darkness, make a swift dash for the sea . . . which they locate by the reflection of moonlight and starlight on the water. Now, nearly twenty years later, some of those hatchlings have hopefully reached adulthood. The group with which I saw my first olive ridley is still active. It has been joined by other organizations and they all work for the conservation of these fascinating marine animals.

All this and more effort will be required to counter new threats on the horizon. In Orissa, several ports have been planned along the coast, such as Dhamra. This is less than ten kilometres from Gahirmatha, a major nesting site for the ridleys. Offshore oil exploration poses another threat. This coastal development, with attendant problems of pollution, lighting, and habitat loss due to changes in beach dynamics, are sure to cause even further declines in the populations. Not only will sea turtles and other marine organisms suffer, but so will the people who depend on marine resources for their livelihoods. Often, such development does not help local people as much as it is expected to do.

Sea turtles are only one of many many species that are threatened by human activity. Will they survive into the next century? That depends on us. If you live near the coast, find out which species of sea turtle nests on those beaches, and join efforts to save them. They need all the help they can get.

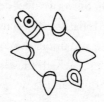

Playtime in the Jungle

Bittu Sahgal

What fun the otters were having! As I watched in wondrous amazement, one, then another and yet another would come whooshing down the slippery mud bank to land—splash!—into the river. Seconds later the energetic scamps would poke their snouts up from under the water, shake their heads to throw a shower of droplets all round (just like wet dogs might) and then clamber up the mud bank again, only to repeat their lightning slide back down into the river. They were young otters, no more than a few months old, and I was sure that their protective mother was not far, though I couldn't see her. Suddenly, the happy squeaking sounds of the young otters turned to excited barks and yelps as they spied their mother, with a huge fish in her mouth, swimming up to the bank less than ten feet from where I lay hidden behind some bushes. It must have taken the hungry litter less than a minute to polish off the silvery fish, bones and all. Meanwhile, the mother quickly slid away to hunt for more fish to feed her bouncy babies.

In all my years of observing animals in the wild, one of the most fascinating sights has been to watch them at play. Scientists and naturalists define 'play' as voluntary activity without any 'real' purpose such as hunting or building a home. At first no one quite knew why animals played at all. After all, play uses up energy and would make them hungry. And food is not exactly easy to come by in a jungle where danger lurks around every corner. Now, however, after years of study by naturalists who want to know why animals do what they do, we have come to the conclusion that play, in the early years of animals' lives, helps them to prepare for survival later. Play, in other words, is the animal equivalent of 'going to school'. Without knowing it, the otters were learning to become master survivors. Later in life these swimming abilities would determine whether or not they would be able to catch the quicksilver fish on which their survival would depend.

*

The three tiger cubs lay scattered around the grass half asleep. Suddenly, one of them, a male, the largest of the lot, pricked up his ears and began to crawl, his belly touching the ground, towards his two lazy sisters. When he was about four or five feet from them, he pounced right on to them and I heard the most wailing cat-like screeches, mixed with hissing and snarling sounds. 'My gosh,' I thought, 'they're fighting.' Within seconds, however, the male retreated without having hurt his sisters in any way. They continued to play 'tag' as one of the cubs ran ahead with a small piece of meat in its mouth, while the other gave chase. Within months of being born, the cubs' 'play' had already taken the shape of stalking 'prey', and the rough and tumble scrapping had begun to train them for the toughness they would need in later years.

*

A commotion high up in a banyan tree, and I was literally 'bombed' with a soft overripe fruit while I was in the middle of my lunch. Looking up, I saw that a troop of grey langurs had wandered into the rest-house compound and I was sitting smack in the middle of their favourite playground. I hurriedly swallowed my meal and sat back quietly as the jungle acrobats put on a fantastic tamasha for me. Some of the older females, who look after the young ones in a troop, were feeding on a nearby tree, while others were sunning themselves or picking lice out of each other's bodies and then promptly eating them up. Three of the langurs that were swinging and pushing and tugging at each other, only a few yards from where I sat, were no more than a couple of months old. Their fur was darker than that of the adults, and their movements more clumsy.

All of a sudden, as though in slow motion, a most peculiar thing happened. One little black fellow was hanging on to a very thin branch about fifteen feet above the ground. Before he could get a proper grip, a second tiny terror, the goonda of the lot, jumped up and caught the poor little guy's tail! This was just too much for the thin branch, and it broke. Down came both rascals, screaming with fright, to land with a plop and a thud almost on me. To top it all, both the young ones and their guardians seemed to feel that I was responsible for this minor catastrophe and I got a real scolding—monkey-style—bared teeth, angry looks, gruff barks and all. No one was hurt, of course, and minutes later the three stooges were back at their swinging and hide-and-seek games. As social animals, the langurs were learning more than mere acrobatic skills. Goonda, for instance, was definitely the leader, and by forcing his will on the others, a sort of pattern was forming for a future langur society where the weaker members would obey a stronger leader. This way they would learn to live as a family, sharing food and shelter and fighting off enemies in the spirit of 'all for one and one for all'. And yet, it looked like so much fun that I actually envied the langurs. They were a carefree, happy-go-lucky bunch of animals at peace with themselves and their environment.

Animal play takes three basic forms. First, the play of an animal by itself, alone, with no companions with whom to interact. I have seen a young deer, for example, jumping, running, rolling in the grass, attacking a low branch with its newly sprouted antlers or splashing around in the shallows of a small pond. Single monkeys or colts often play alone like this too, as though to let off steam. The second form of play is social, the kind our friends the langurs and the tiger cubs were participating in. No one gets hurt, but many lessons are learned by these play-fights. The third, a very interesting kind of play, takes place when an animal uses 'toys'. Yes, it's true. Chimps, for instance, throw sticks around, or break large leaves off trees to dip them in water, eventually splashing some around and drinking some by licking the leaves. This teaches them to use tools.

As animals grow older, they tend to play less. And, for some reason, male animals tend to spend more time playing than the females of their species. Once I was witness to some really rough play between two nearly full-grown jackals. From the sounds they were making and their snarling lips and bared teeth, I thought one would surely kill the other. However, this was not to be. At what could be some pre-determined signal, one of the jackals rolled over on his back and started making whimpering sounds as if to say, 'Enough! Enough! You win. Now let's play a gentle game.' The stronger jackal stopped his attack immediately, but as though to prove his superiority, he went to a nearby bush, lifted a leg and sprayed it with some urine. Later in the jackal's life, this same scent-marking habit would be the language by which he would tell other jackals to stay away from 'his' part of the jungle.

As each day passes, scientists come up with new theories of how animals evolved and why some became more clever than others. These days, some scientists are suggesting that

Homo sapiens (that's the scientific name for humans) may have developed a clever brain because early in his evolution he discovered the joys of play! No one can be one hundred per cent sure, of course, but their theories sound quite reasonable. They suggest that early man probably threw things like sticks or stones either at each other or at other animals to frighten them. Slowly, they must have discovered how useful such 'toys' were as missiles to bring down small animals or birds. Play, therefore, could possibly have helped humans to become hunters. Then, by using signals and sounds, men discovered that they could produce reactions in their fellow men—either happiness, or fear, or even reassurance. Years of 'fooling around' with such signs probably led to the birth of man's sophisticated language.

One thing that has emerged from the study of play in the animal world is the fact that the more 'intelligent' the species and the more free-ranging (wandering) its habits, the more it tends to play. Thus, play has commonly been observed among creatures as diverse as dolphins, orcas, whales, river otters, elephants, polar bears, chimpanzees, ravens, parrots and, of course, humans. The sophistication of human play has taken unbelievable leaps in recent years. With the invention of the micro-chip, the television and the computer, children are learning the principles of aerodynamics, sonar, battle-tactics and plain simple reading, writing and arithmetic at a much younger age than their elders ever did. In fact, most teachers who specialize in guiding young children through their critical growing years are coming to the conclusion that the new sophisticated forms of play we see today are likely to lead us towards our next giant evolutionary leap—the discovery of the power of the mind.

The Magic Ring

Zai Whitaker

Dr Salim Ali, the Birdman of India, is one of the world's most famous naturalists. His Book of Indian Birds *has become a classic. With little money and none of the slick equipment naturalists use today, he revolutionized bird study and made many discoveries about their natural history and behaviour. He played a major part in conserving bird habitats. This chapter, about his bird migration studies, is from the book* Salim Ali for Schools.

Early naturalists spent a lot of time scratching their heads and wondering. They did not have the solid body of scientific work that we have today. We can trot off to a library and find out about something as remote as, say, the bushmaster of South America or the megapode of Papua New Guinea. Or we can get on the Internet and go click-click-click and read the latest scientific discoveries about otters and ostriches, elephants and eels. But that was not always so. In fact it is only in the last hundred years that the secrets about birds and animals have been unlocked.

One of the mysteries that caused much head-scratching and mumbling through learned beards was bird migration. Large flocks of thousands of birds left a place and came back a year later around the same time, sometimes on the very same day. Where did they go and how did they find their way back? Some early naturalists believed they hid in the bottom of the sea, to rise like the Phoenix in the Greek legend.

Of course, scientific study and discovery had progressed much further by the time Salim Ali arrived on the scene. By then, naturalists knew that many species of birds, big and small, fly thousands of miles every year to escape cold winters, and to lay their eggs and raise their chicks in the comfort of a warm land. After all, who wants to be in Siberia in winter? Like all tourists, birds want warmth and good food and a comfortable place (at reasonable prices). Some fly 11,000 miles—each way—to and from their winter resting place.

But how do birds find their way to a specific spot on the other side of the world, year after year? Like computer-programmed objects, they fly thousands of miles and land at a particular lake or forest or river, every year. Their timing, too, is perfect: migrants are extremely punctual, unlike many of us, and arrive within a day or two of their previous year's arrival. Without watches or computers or travel agents, how do they do it? Why don't they lose their way, or die of exhaustion?

It was once thought that migration was a 'taught' behaviour, and that bird parents guided their young on these long journeys. But in many species of birds, the young make their first migratory journey alone, without mum and dad. Salim often gave the example of the cuckoo in Europe, and he once told a journalist:

'The cuckoo is what is called a brood-parasite. It lays its eggs in the nests of other species, and just forgets about it. The young are hatched out and brought up by the foster parents. Now, in the UK, the cuckoo, soon after laying its eggs, migrates to Africa. The young are brought up by foster parents who themselves are non-migratory birds. They do not migrate and therefore they cannot teach their foster birdlings anything about migration. Yet, remarkably enough, as soon as the young cuckoo is able to fly, it flies off to join its parents in Africa—as much as 6,500 kilometres away.'

Migration is therefore not a behaviour which is taught by parents. It is caused by strong genetic or inborn instincts which all animals—from mollusks to elephants—share. Like a good computer program, instinct guides them to food and friends, and prevents them from getting lost as they roam miles and miles in different directions.

There are two seasons of bird 'travel' to and from India every year. Millions of birds belonging to about 300 species fly thousands of miles to get to their nesting places, and return in the spring when the weather warms up. A flock of migrating birds, sometimes several thousands strong, is an unforgettable sight. This is also the time when otherwise solitary birds are seen together. The marsh harrier, for example, is usually seen individually or in pairs, but during a survey in Afghanistan, Salim Ali saw a large flock of them arriving and settling in a ploughed field as it was getting dark. Having come all the way from India, they were obviously exhausted. But they were off again at daybreak.

By the 1960s, ornithologists in many countries had begun studying bird migration by ringing birds. Salim made a start with his team from the Bombay Natural History Society. A small aluminum or plastic ring—too small and light to handicap the bird—is clamped on the bird's foot. On the ring is a message asking the finder of the bird to return the ring to a particular address, such as the BNHS. He is also asked to name the place, date and time the bird was found. As a young man, Salim had participated in bird-ringing camps in Heligoland, Germany, and this had given him useful training. A few trial bird-ringing camps around Mumbai, and their results, showed that it should be done on a larger scale. But there was the usual, small problem. Money. For a while it looked pretty unhopeful. But in the end it worked out, thanks, funnily enough, to a lowly virus.

A strange viral disease had broken out in Shimoga district of Karnataka state, and was affecting humans and monkeys. It was new to Indian doctors and no one could figure out exactly what it was, and how to cure it. It became even more mysterious when scientists at the Pune Virus Research Centre, peering through their microscopes, discovered it came from Western Siberia. There, it caused a disease known as Russian Spring-Summer Encephalitis, very much like the Shimoga sickness. But how did this Siberian virus get to Karnataka?

The World Health Organization (WHO) wanted to find out, and it asked Salim and the BNHS for help. Perhaps the ticks and other parasites carrying this virus had come from Siberia. Could migratory birds be the culprits? Many winter migrants in Indian came from Siberia, so it was likely. Well, Salim was only too happy to find out, and he was invited to a WHO meeting in Geneva to make all the arrangements. And in this way bird ringing (or bird banding) began in India. Salim and his team would certainly collect ticks and other parasites for the WHO. At the same time, he would be able to clamp on the magic ring that would tell the story of bird migration to and from India.

The first area chosen for setting up a bird-ringing camp was the Rann of Kutch. (This is the desert that was hit by the terrible earthquake on 26 January 2001.) Why, of all places, the uncomfortable desert of Kutch? Many of our winter bird visitors come from northwestern lands like Eastern Europe and Siberia. To avoid flying over the skyscraper peaks of the Himalayas, they come in through the Indus valley and 'turn left' into the land blob of the Gujarat peninsula. So, in 1960, Salim and other ornithologists from the BNHS were in the desert, setting up nets in preparation for the first wave of migrant birds.

They had already received a few very startling 'recoveries' (rings returned to the BNHS), even from faraway Turkestan and Siberia. Ornithologists all over the world were becoming serious bird-ringers, and the technology had advanced. The early nets to trap the birds had been heavy and difficult to manage. Since then, the Japanese had invented 'mist nets', which were light and springy, like giant spider webs.

Next question: where should these nets be put up? A place had to be found where the migrants would 'picnic' for a day or two, to rest, eat and drink before their next long flight. Done. But as soon as the tents were pitched and the camp got going, there was a sudden, heavy, early monsoon, bringing flood and famine. It was difficult to work in that large swamp, or even to find food for the bird team.

But the success of this camp was that the ornithologists from the BNHS learned to use the mist nets. An expert had especially come from Switzerland to show them how to put up the long, almost invisible nets on bamboo poles. Even the keen eyesight of birds missed its hair-thin strands of nylon. Imagining it is flying into a bush, or patch of grass, the bird finds itself bouncing about in a hammock. Being springy and elastic, the net doesn't damage the bird. But it must be quickly untangled, weighed, measured, and ringed. Then it is free to fly away, wondering what on earth that noise and excitement was all about.

The camp was a real bird haven, but unfortunately it was

also a favourite spot for snakes. It was infested by saw-scaled vipers, deadly venomous snakes which move fast and are quick to strike. The snake's sandy colouring makes it blend in so well with the desert soil that it's easy to step on. Salim had brought along an antivenom serum kit, and on the first evening they tried to follow the instructions. But they were so complicated that it was decided that in case of a bite, they should be kind to the victim and allow him to die peacefully! Fortunately, no one was bitten in spite of some close shaves.

These bird-ringing camps became an important part of the work of Dr Salim Ali and the Bombay Natural History Society. Millions of birds were ringed in many parts of the country, and the 'recoveries' began to tell, for the first time, the story of where and how migrants fly. The chief and most important ringing centre was Keoladeo near Bharatpur in Rajasthan, which is today a national park thanks to Salim's campaign for its conservation. It is a large wetland where millions of migrant waterfowl and other birds arrive every winter. One of these is the rare and beautiful Siberian crane. It is also home to many species of water birds, such as storks, herons, spoonbills and ibises, which breed here and then migrate locally, within India; they are 'domestic tourists'. Very little was known about their movements as well.

This bird paradise was the private hunting ground of the royal family of Bharatpur. Their VIP guests were 'entertained' by mass massacres of water birds which were kept moving by beaters, making them easy targets. There are records of three and four thousand birds shot in a single day! But the real danger to Bharatpur came after Independence when the local farmers and politicians tried, and almost succeeded, in getting this fantastic birdhouse drained and converted into agricultural land.

This would have been the end of one of the most precious water-bird havens in the world. Fortunately Salim, who knew Prime Minister Nehru personally and also knew of his deep love for nature, asked him to stop this crazy plan. And Nehru did. Today ornithologists and tourists come from all over the world to watch the teeming bird life of Keoladeo National Park.

Notes on Contributors

American naturalist **Dr Clifford G. Rice** was born in India. His interest in wildlife grew out of childhood experiences in Madhya Pradesh, Uttaranchal, and Punjab. In addition to his doctoral research on Nilgiri tahr, he was a Peace Corps volunteer in Nepal, and coordinated a study on the sloth bear in Madhya Pradesh. He has also been a biologist for the Commonwealth of the Northern Mariana Islands and the U.S. Army (endangered species conservation on military lands). Most recently, he has done research on mountain goats in Washington State, USA.

Ashish Chandola was born and brought up in Dehra Dun in the foothills of the Himalayas, where he also went to school.

His early enthusiasm for natural history and photography was fostered and encouraged by his parents and teachers at school. This interest, indeed fascination, brought him in contact with some of the great people involved with wildlife conservation. After a stint at a jungle lodge in Nepal as a naturalist, he taught himself wildlife photography and his hobby became his career. He has made several wildlife films, most of them in India.

Dr Monica Jackson grew up in Honnametti, a coffee estate in the Biligiri hills near Mysore. Like her father Ralph Morris, she became madly interested in the wildlife, forest and people of that area. As a student at Cambridge and Edinburgh Universities, she did her doctoral thesis on Caste, Culture and Human fertility in Chamarajnagar, Karnataka. Monica is also a mountaineer and has been on expeditions in the Himalayas, Alps, Dolomites, Turkish Kurdistan and the Atlas Mountains of Morocco. Her books include *Tents in the Clouds*, *The Turkish Time Machine*, and *Going Back*. She now lives in Edinburgh, Scotland.

Dr Ramachandra Guha is a social, environmental and cricket historian and biographer. He is also a wonderful speaker and much in demand both on television and in real life. He has held many academic positions at universities including Yale, Stanford, Oslo, and the Indian Institute of Science. His books include *Environmentalism: A Global History*, *Savaging the Civilized: Verrier Elwin, His Tribals, and India*, and, most recently, *India after Gandhi: The History of the World's Largest Democracy*. Among the numerous awards and recognition he has received are the R.K. Narayan Prize, MacArthur Research and Writing Award, and the Leopold-Hidy Prize of the American Society for Environmental History.

Rom Whitaker came to India with his family in 1951 when he was seven years old. His mother encouraged his interest in snakes and other reptiles, which grew into a lifelong passion. Rom started India's first reptile park and helped the Irula snake-catching tribe set up their own 'venom cooperative'. He has written extensively on the subject of reptiles and published several books. Also a film-maker, he has produced and presented several documentaries and a children's feature film. At the moment, Rom is trying to save the endangered gharial from extinction.

Dr George Schaller is very lucky: he has spent over fifty years studying wildlife in many parts of the world. He works with the Wildlife Conservation Society in New York. This has given him the freedom to study gorillas in the Congo and lions in Tanzania. He came to India to learn about the life of tigers and went to Pakistan in search of snow leopards. For a long time now he has worked in China high on the Tibetan Plateau to help protect animals like the wild yak and Tibetan antelope. The purpose of this, and many other studies, is to collect the kind of information that will help protect these beautiful animals.

Ian Lockwood is a teacher, writer and photographer, with an insatiable fascination for South Asia. Originally from Boston in the USA, he grew up in Bangladesh's sal forests and spent his formative years exploring the Palni Hills instead of preparing for classes and the serious business of life. He has a special interest in tropical forests, obscure mountain peaks and the endemic creatures of the Western Ghats. His black and white photographs of the Western Ghats have been widely admired and displayed.

Sally R. Walker migrated from the USA to India in order to improve her health through yogasana study… which she did for seven years, until Mysore Zoo's tiger cubs distracted her. At Mysore Zoo, she saw how well-managed zoos could generate sympathy for wildlife and communicate information on environmental issues. In order to help zoos improve animal care and visitor behaviour, as well as breed endangered species, Sally started several organizations, including Friends of Mysore Zoo, the Zoo Outreach Organization, and the South Asian Zoo Organization. In 2004, she received the highest award in the zoo professional community, the World Zoo Association's Heini Heidigger Award

Manish Chandi studied economics at Madras Christian College, but then realized this wasn't really what he wanted to do. Looking for adventure and commitment, he went to the Andaman Islands as a volunteer for the Madras Crocodile Bank and WWF India in 1995 and became 'hooked' to this amazing ecosystem. He surveyed mangrove creeks for crocodiles and beaches for sea turtles, camping on remote beaches and staying with native islanders. He got to know the people of Little Nicobar Island, and their unique culture. Manish's work has contributed to the understanding and conservation of the Andaman and Nicobar archipelago, which is being rapidly destroyed by unsuitable tourism, welfare and industrial projects.

Born in Chennai, **Shanthi Chandola** did her schooling in Kolkata. Interested in forests and wildlife, she worked as a naturalist at various wildlife resorts in India. Keen on making wildlife films, she got her big break when she worked on the BBC mega series, *Land of the Tiger*. Together with her husband Ashish and the photographer TNA Perumal, Shanthi recently compiled and edited a book of photographs and writings of the pioneer naturalist, M. Krishnan. Shanthi and Ashish are based in Bangalore, and are involved with organic farming and nature photography besides making the occasional wildlife film.

Dr Kartik Shanker stumbled upon a career in ecology after watching a nesting olive ridley turtle on a beach in Chennai. He helped establish the Students' Sea Turtle Conservation Network. After his Ph.D on small mammals, he began a study on sea turtle genetics. He now works on the biology and conservation of sea turtles throughout their habitat, including Orissa and the Andaman and Nicobar Islands. He is Assistant Professor at the Centre for Ecological Sciences, Indian Institute of Science, Bangalore and heads the Coastal and Marine Programme at ATREE, Bangalore.

Bittu Sahgal is the editor of *Sanctuary* magazine and the founder of Kids for Tigers, the Sanctuary Tiger Programme. He believes that children have the power to force adults to 'do the right thing' for our planet and our country. His life revolves around campaigns to save the wildlife of India and its forest home. He has also written hundreds of articles about Indian wildlife and conservation. He is working with others to impress upon Indian leaders the need to take the climate change threat more seriously.